LOUISIANA
TECH'S
JOE
AILLET

LOUISIANA TECH'S
JOE AILLET

CHRISTOPHER A. KENNEDY

THE
History
PRESS

Published by The History Press
Charleston, SC
www.historypress.com

Cover image: Joe Aillet at his office in Memorial Gymnasium, circa 1960s. *From the Louisiana Tech Sports Communication Department.*

First published 2022

Manufactured in the United States

ISBN 9781467152334

Library of Congress Control Number: 2022936636

Notice: The information in this book is true and complete to the best of our knowledge. It is offered without guarantee on the part of the author or The History Press. The author and The History Press disclaim all liability in connection with the use of this book.

To my parents. To Selene, who suggested I visit Cynthia Aillet Murry, the daughter of Joe Aillet, and to Gary, who accompanied me to Holy Cross High School and St. Edward's University. Thank you for your support throughout the adventure.

CONTENTS

FOREWORD

Every day, as I take the short drive to my office, I pass by a sign that says "Joe Aillet."

Over the past fifty years, thousands of people have passed by that sign daily, many wondering why Joe Aillet deserved to have his name imprinted on the football stadium that stands prominently in the gateway to Louisiana Tech University.

I arrived on campus as a student fifty years ago, just a few months after Joe Aillet passed away. I never met him personally, but I learned much about him over the years. His children and later generations of the family have been close friends, and I have known many of the student-athletes he coached and many others who knew him. In his time at Louisiana Tech, Coach Aillet became a prominent leader on the football field, a teacher and a talented and brilliant mentor for hundreds.

Louisiana Tech graduate Christopher Kennedy was one of those who sought out Coach Aillet's story. In this volume, Christopher shares both historical documents and personal interviews about the improbable life's journey of an orphan in New York who rose to be a tremendously impactful leader in the Deep South.

This work provides great insights into those people who shaped Joe Aillet's life, including his adopted family, his church, his colleagues and his coaching mentors. Christopher also shares the perspectives of so many people who were positively affected by Coach Aillet.

Joe Aillet established a strong culture within his team, on campus and in his profession that remains evident today. He was highly respected and attracted many talented and successful student-athletes and coaches to Louisiana Tech during his tenure. Loyalty is one of the Tenets of Tech—an integral value and part of our institutional culture, reinforced daily on the Louisiana Tech campus. Coach Aillet served as the embodiment of that value for many here. He kept his commitment to remain at Louisiana Tech despite many opportunities elsewhere over his career, and he instilled this commitment in hundreds of members of the Tech Family during his service to our university.

Coach Aillet also had a significant social impact in this community. Christopher shares unique insights into how Aillet brought Catholicism into a deeply rooted Protestant community, making the community more diverse and welcoming to a broader population. Today, many Catholic students attend Louisiana Tech because of the foundation established by Joe Aillet. Christopher Kennedy was one of those.

Christopher tells the story of Joe Aillet's success as a coach. More importantly, he conveys the influence of a man who lived his life and created a strong legacy without knowing his own roots. Coach Aillet ensured that those he coached would have their names enshrined in halls of fame and inscribed on the walls of boardrooms. He had as much impact on a small university in North Louisiana as anyone in its first century. We have those who ran an orphan train—and those individuals who shared their homes with those children—to thank for that.

DR. LES GUICE,
President, Louisiana Tech University

PREFACE

J oe Aillet's unique background has periodically been brought to attention in the years after his passing and continues to intrigue the public. Fewer people today know about the orphan trains of previous centuries. His upbringing by Eliza Aillet and the years of education spent with the Congregation of Holy Cross allowed for a strong and fortunate foundation. Aillet honored his adoptive family and the Holy Cross family by his life's work—building successful football and golf teams, athletes and men. He worked with coaches of exemplary caliber and successfully kept their services. This book brings to light his story and sets the record straight.

ACKNOWLEDGEMENTS

Special thanks to Cynthia Aillet Murry. Without her cooperation and enthusiasm, this book would not have been written. Also, thanks to the interviewees and those from the Opelousas Orphan Train Museum, Holy Cross School, St. Edward's University, University of Louisiana at Lafayette, Northwestern State University, Louisiana Tech University, St. Thomas Aquinas Catholic Church, the Louisiana State Archives and the many individuals whose assistance and encouragement helped make this possible.

CHAPTER 1

A NEW YORK CHILD
FINDS HIS HOME

New York, May 1907. A train whistle beckons to a new future shrouded in its mysterious steam as several children led by Catholic sisters board the railcars. They may be orphans now, but they would cease to be by the end of the trip.

The story of Joe Aillet begins, oddly enough, not in South Louisiana but in New York City. Born on September 14, 1904, Aillet was not Cajun but rather was from a humble immigrant background. Not much is known about his biological parents. His mother was Irish, the granddaughter of a woman who came to the United States to escape the Great Famine. Little is known about his father other than his name was Joseph Fourka.

Because his family could not take care of him,[1] Aillet was given to the New York Foundling Hospital, a Catholic institution dating back to the late nineteenth century. The hospital was founded by Catherine Rosamond Fitzgibbons (Sister Mary Irene) of the Sisters of Charity of New York, a religious order founded by St. Elizabeth Ann Seaton.[2]

Cities on the East Coast swelled with immigrants arriving in America for numerous reasons, such as religious toleration, escaping political repression and job availability. Often, there were not enough jobs to go around, and some groups, such as the Irish, faced discrimination. Poverty, overcrowding, unsanitary conditions and a financial crisis shortly before the Civil War adversely affected the well-being of these immigrant families. Children were orphaned for any number of reasons, such as disease, starvation and parents' addictions. Other children were abandoned. Some lived in the streets; others were given to rich families or left in tenements or convents.

These horrid conditions for immigrants persisted long into the future in cities such as New York.[3]

The NYFH, founded in 1869, joined older institutions such as the New York Juvenile Asylum (now Children's Village) and the Children's Aid Society (now Children's Aid) in using the orphan train system. Early pioneers, such as Reverend Charles Brace, began the system in 1854—widely seen as a precursor to modern adoption and foster care systems of today. Orphan trains operated until 1929, carrying an estimated 250,000 children across North America.[4]

Joe Aillet's family had him baptized at St. Bernard's Catholic Church in New York. His mother, when she gave him to the sisters at the NYFH, said that she was unable to take care of him and prayed that they would see that he was adopted by a good family who would love him and give him the things they were not able to give him.

The NYFH was highly respected, especially among the Catholic communities that benefited from the services of the sisters. Though far from a perfect system, they succeeded in sending thousands of children to new homes. Parish priests were crucial to the program; they publicized the "baby trains," preaching the mission during sermons at Mass. If there was sufficient interest in the congregation, a fleet of orphan trains was requested. Priests commonly worked with married couples who were trusted to be suitable parents. Families could request a baby based on physical characteristics such as hair color, eye color, skin tone and sex—the idea being that the children would be raised in as "familiar" an environment as possible. Layman agents were also used to assist priests and periodically check in on children once they had been settled with a family.[5]

Joe Aillet's journey to Louisiana was unique. A priest from Youngsville, a small town near Lafayette, came to visit the NYFH shortly before it would be Aillet's turn to ride the trains. Father Johanni Rouget, pastor of St. Anne's Catholic Church, toured the facility. This was not uncommon. Father John Engerbrink of St. Landry's Catholic Church in Opelousas, Louisiana, also toured the facility; it was he who organized the orphan trains that came to Opelousas.[6] When Father Rouget visited, he found Joseph Fourka, who was widely known in the Foundling Hospital for being a handsome and intelligent baby. He immediately made what would become a lifelong impression on Father Rouget.

Upon returning to Youngsville, Father Rouget began publicizing for the orphan train. Several families in the area were interested, including the Aillet family.

Father Johanni Rouget with his pets. *From Cynthia Aillet Murry.*

On May 7, 1907, an orphan train fleet containing three cars full of children arrived in Opelousas, twenty-nine miles north of Lafayette. Some two thousand children came to Louisiana on the orphan trains; some arrived in New Orleans, others in Morgan City, Lafayette, Opelousas and Mansura.[7]

The children, accompanied by sisters, met their new families; they wore tags with numbers corresponding to the ones their new family had. Many children encountered a language barrier with their new families; often, their primary language was not French, the primary language spoken by families of the area. Because these children were young, they adapted more easily to Cajun culture. It was common for children when riding the NYFH's baby trains to be two to six years old; Joe Aillet was two and a half.

Joseph Fourka's new adopted name became Joseph Rouget Aillet (the middle name in honor of Father Rouget). His adoptive family included his new parents, Joseph Numa Aillet and Eliza Lefebvre Aillet, and five siblings: Clarence, Travis, Celeste, Maud and Lydia. Joseph Numa died in 1909 two years after Aillet's adoption, leaving Eliza to take care of him. As was customary, his adoption was not discussed with him. He only found out about his adoption accidentally. While still a child but old enough to run errands, he was sent to the neighborhood store one day. It happened to be while a family picture was being made. When he returned, he realized what had happened. Confused and upset, he sat on the doorstep outside crying. Clarence came outside and sat with him. Trying to comfort his brother, he explained about Joe's adoption. It is unclear, however, how much detail he went into. It is likely he did not talk about the orphan train. In fact, it would be much later that Aillet discovered his whole story, again thanks to Clarence.[8]

CHAPTER 2

A HOLY CROSS EDUCATION

Fortunately for Joe Aillet, he was taken in by a loving family and treated well. Father Rouget, the man most responsible for Aillet arriving in Youngsville, was a busy man. His church parish was a growing one, yet it was still profoundly rural. Although he remained intensely active, Father Rouget never forgot about his young friend. He wrote notes on Aillet to keep track of him and would aid Aillet in getting into Holy Cross School in New Orleans.[9]

In 1916, a twelve-year-old Aillet entered Holy Cross and attended through high school. At that time, Holy Cross operated as a boarding school. He remained on campus while in school, only coming home on certain holidays such as Christmas.[10] Holy Cross, along with the universities of Notre Dame and St. Edward's, would have a profound effect on young Aillet's life.

Holy Cross was operated by the Congregation of Holy Cross, a religious order founded in Le Mans, France, in 1837. The official Latinized name of Congregation of Holy Cross is Congregation a Santa Cruce, or CSC. Its mission was education, and it founded schools and universities. The beginning of its mission to North America saw its headquarters established in the small but growing town of South Bend, Indiana. In 1841–42, a group of six brothers and one priest entered Indiana, settled in South Bend after being invited by Bishop Célestine Hailandière of Vincennes and established Notre Dame University, the oldest continuously operated school of CSC in the world.[11] In 1849, five brothers and three sisters of CSC were requested to travel to New Orleans by Bishop Antoine Blanc (archbishop the following year) to take ownership of St. Mary's Orphanage. The institution that Joe Aillet would later attend was, as fate would have it, originally an orphanage not unlike the NYFH; both served orphaned Catholic immigrant children. In keeping with a strong athletic emphasis of CSC institutions, it also provided a solid football base for Aillet before attending St. Edward's.

For the rest of the century, Holy Cross continued to take shape as a school. St. Isidore's College was founded in 1879. In 1896, it became known as Holy Cross. Finally, in 1912, it shifted its focus to secondary education. Aillet was eight years old. Brother Engelbert Leisse, CSC, became the first brother president (headmaster) of Holy Cross College, among other duties, and would remain so until Joe Aillet's senior year, when Leisse was transferred to Notre Dame. By his senior year, the school had achieved its highest enrollment up to that point.[12]

Aillet's time at Holy Cross no doubt had a profound impact on him. The mission of CSC was to provide education to those in need. In the words of the order's founder, Blessed Basil Moreau, "We can state in a word the kind of teaching we wish to impart. We do not want our students to be ignorant of anything they should know. To this end, we shall avoid no sacrifice. We shall always place education side by side with instruction: the mind will not be cultivated at the expense of the heart. While we prepare useful citizens for society, we shall likewise do our utmost to prepare citizens for eternal life."[13]

Attending Holy Cross School proved monumental for Joe Aillet. Moreau's Holy Cross is concerned with "[e]ducating the whole man: mind and heart, body and soul."[14] Perhaps the most important areas that Aillet would benefit from the school were spiritually, educationally, musically and athletically.

Aillet was involved in the *Gold and Blue*, an early yearbook, and the Monogram Club. School colors were in imitation of Notre Dame, the first school in the United States run by CSC. He was also a member of the religious groups League of the Sacred Heart and Holy Name Society. As part of the League of the Sacred Heart, every first Friday of the month, students would receive Holy Communion; in the afternoon, they would complete activities "proper to the day." The Holy Name Society usually met at least once a month, where during general meetings, papers of religious work were read and discussed.

Aillet was a five-sport athlete, participating in football, basketball, baseball, track and tennis. Coach Leo Ernst had for two years overseen all athletics at the school, along with manager Brother Godfrey Vallaso, CSC. Above all else, Coach Ernst valued good sportsmanship, tolerating nothing less on his teams.

From 1916, when Aillet first arrived, Holy Cross had a reputation in basketball and baseball. Rules for most sports were different, which led to often lopsided scores unfamiliar to twenty-first-century audiences. His senior year, Aillet was his baseball team's captain. Although they missed some key players from the previous season when they were Prep Champions, they would finish the season with a winning record, in the process beating St. Aloysius (now Brother Martin) and evening the score against Jesuit, 1-1, their chief rivals. Holy Cross suffered one shutout against rival Warren Easton High School and won a shutout against Soule College. Aillet played left field and was acknowledged for his hitting ability at the plate. In basketball, Aillet was listed as a guard. The team had a good start in Prep League play, having similar results against their rivals as they would in baseball, but barely missed becoming league champions. Every game they lost was close. Of twenty-one games, thirteen were played at home; the only home loss was at the hands of Marine Bank. A shutout was won against Rugby Academy.

Unfortunately, his mother, Eliza, died in 1922. While this saddened Aillet, it was also the inaugural season of football at Holy Cross. It is ironic for Aillet, whose future was destined in the sport, to only start playing his senior year. Several eager students tried out and made the team. Aillet was listed as a fullback on offense—no defensive designation was given, although most players played both ways. The new team's colors were Notre Dame green and gold and went by the nickname of the "Micks."[15]

Football, of all sports, had some major differences in the 1922–23 season as compared to modern football. Holy Cross's twenty-man squad, small by today's standards, was average for the time. Also, while today's high school football teams have several players who are at least two hundred pounds, high school players in the '20s weighed significantly less. Often, only thirteen to fourteen players took snaps in a game. Because the shape of the ball was more round and less wieldy than modern footballs, along with rules greatly limiting the potential for forward passes, running plays were far more prevalent. Coaching from the sideline during a game was prohibited, as it was seen as poor sportsmanship. Only players, usually the team captain, could call plays. Statistics of prep school games were often not diligently kept.[16]

It proved to be a rough inaugural season for Holy Cross, as the Micks were 2-4-1. Every game, with two exceptions, was a shutout one way or the other. In the game against St. Aloysius, Joe Aillet scored a PAT in the 13–0 victory. The illegal sideline coaching rule of the time came into play when, in the fourth quarter, a sub came into the huddle and spoke to the quarterback of SA. Because of this, the Saints received a 15-yard penalty.[17] Another notable game of the season was a defeat at the hands of Jesuit. Although the Micks suffered a grievous loss against Jesuit, Aillet recovered a fumble on defense. This was the beginning of one of New Orleans' most heated rivalries, for as Holy Cross "look[ed] for a bright future on the gridiron,"[18] these teams would often find themselves vying not only for regional bragging rights but also bragging rights at the state level.

For all of Joe Aillet's involvement at Holy Cross, perhaps the most evident example of his leadership was being elected class president. He made many lifelong friends at Holy Cross; John Lynch would become the third head football coach at Holy Cross after he graduated in 1926 and would reconnect with Aillet in the future. In no small way, the Holy Cross experience would serve to profoundly shape the person he was to become. Aillet's senior quote fits his character: "As welcome as sunshine in every place—so the beaming approval of a good-natured face."

CHAPTER 3

COLLEGE YEARS

After graduating from Holy Cross, Joe Aillet would attend another Notre Dame–linked educational institution, St. Edward's University in Austin, Texas. Accompanying him was classmate and team captain of the Holy Cross football team George Schloegel.

St. Edward's experienced a very similar founding as Holy Cross. Bishop Claude M. Dubuis of Galveston requested that CSC build a Catholic school in Texas. In 1871, Mary Doyle, widow of James Doyle, willed 398 acres near Austin for the building of a Catholic school. Father Edward Sorin, superior general of CSC, founded St. Edward's Academy in 1877, which became St. Edward's College in 1885. It would not become a university until 1925, when Aillet was a junior. The institution was named in honor of Father Edward's patron saint, King Edward the Confessor of England. Father Edward, one of the earliest members of CSC, was the priest who, accompanied by the five brothers, settled in South Bend and founded Notre Dame.[19]

Aillet enjoyed and appreciated his time at St. Edward's, or "St. Ed's." Unsurprisingly, many of his activities carried over to his new school. He was a member of the Knights of Columbus, a Catholic fraternal service order. Aillet was elected the sophomore class president in 1924 and, in the same year, served as the vice-chair of the Student's Activities Committee, a group tasked with organizing the social events of the school.

Team colors were again Notre Dame gold and blue. As St. Edward's was the "Notre Dame of the Southwest," many of Aillet's teammates would go on to play or coach at Notre Dame. He played baseball and basketball, as well as football. John "Jack" Meagher coached all sports and served as athletic director. A Notre Dame graduate, Meagher played football in the one-loss 1916 season as an end when Notre Dame legend Knute Rockne was an assistant; he made honorable mention in Walter Camp's All-American team before serving in World War I in the Marine Corps when the United States entered the next year. After a brief stint with the Chicago Tigers in the first year of the National Football League in 1920, Meagher became head coach of St. Ed's in 1921; his teams suffered only three losses from 1923 to 1925 and had an undefeated season in '23. As a "maker of men,"[20] Coach Meagher's direction

Coach Jack Meagher. *From the St. Edward's Tower, 1925.*

would serve as another beneficial development of Aillet as an athlete and as a person. Meagher would go on to become the head coach of Rice, Auburn and the Miami Seahawks and reappear in Aillet's life multiple times.

Aillet played as a quarterback and punt returner on offense and an end on defense. Every year he lettered. His freshman season was during the remarkable, undefeated campaign of 1923. Every game played demonstrated the indomitable spirit of the St. Edward Saints. Anchored by a stalwart defense and a versatile offense, carried over from the previous season, the team was well served. Aillet, while serving as a replacement quarterback for Thornton "Thorny" O'Connor, was "fast and shifty, a clear thinker, and carrie[d] all the good points that a real quarterback should have."[21] Among Aillet's teammates, future Chicago Cardinal halfback Melvin Stuessy, along with left tackle and captain Edmund "Moose" Woeber, future basketball coach of St. Ed's, stood out among a talented field.

Aillet played in the Grubbs Vocational College (now University of Texas at Arlington), Simmons College (now Hardin-Simmons) and Daniel Baker (now Howard Payne University) games, all shutouts, as well as the Thanksgiving Day game at San Antonio against Phillips University (closed). An especially enthusiastic student crowd cheered the Saints underdogs on at the Thanksgiving game.[22] A notable win was against the Baylor Cubs, the freshman team in the second game of the season, 7-2. Called "the best exhibition of football shown in Austin this season," the Saints won a close, tough homecoming matchup. It rained during the second half of the game, slowing things down, and triple-threat back Mel Stuessy sustained an ankle fracture, taking him out for at least five weeks.[23] The next big game resulted in the Saints traveling to another tough opponent, last season's undefeated Tulsa, where the Golden Hurricane was destroyed 35–7. A nonetheless entertaining halftime show of prizewinning Dog Show contestants and high school band performances could not prevent an offensive and defensive dismantling of the home team.[24] One final game for the Saints was played against the San Antonio military base and won, winning 13–12.

St. Edward's, in all athletics but especially in football, looked to compete with the best. The football played by the team, especially in that decade once Coach Meagher claimed the helm, made them known widely as one of the best small college programs in the state. Their reputation as playing a gentlemanly game also preceded them in their contests. Accomplished professional and college football player-coach E.J. "Doc" Stewart, in his first year coaching the University of Texas (also to an undefeated season), heaped lavish praise on the neighboring college: "The highest compliment I can pay your team and your coach is to remark that your team in action reminds me of Notre Dame."[25] When Meagher entered the room during the dinner celebrating the "Notre Dame of the South's" undefeated 1923 season, he was greeted by the rousing cheering of the team.

Several athletes from the football team also played basketball, coached by Meagher. Aillet was a forward and played with skill and spirit to counteract what he lacked in size. Having a hand in a few games, Aillet came off the bench and scored two points in each of the first three games, victories for the Saints. The last game in January was a defeat in a rematch on the home court of Austin College, where Aillet did not score. The '24 basketball team finished the season 11-3.

Aillet left his mark in baseball as well. The opening series of baseball in March 1924 was against newly founded Stephen F. Austin Teacher's College (now Stephen F. Austin State University); the Saints swept the series. Joe Aillet played in the second game, a shutout. April was sprinkled with victories and defeats; Aillet hit a single in a defeat to the Alamo Peck Indians, a team representing a furniture company of that name.[26] Toward the end of the month, three defeats were sustained on the road. The first one was against Louisiana Polytech Institute (now Louisiana Tech University) in a high-scoring affair, 12–9; the second game of that series was rained out. Although Aillet likely did not even imagine it, this was the beginning of a lifelong relationship with Louisiana Tech. The next defeat was at the hands of the Monroe Drillers, a minor-league member of the Cotton States League, in their first season; in front of a large crowd, the Saints failed to achieve a ninth-inning comeback

(3–2). The end of the Louisiana trip occurred in a shutout handed to them by Centenary College (1–0). The series ended as the second game was rained out with the Saints leading 3–1 at the end of the fourth inning.

Excitement was in the air, not only in anticipation for the upcoming 1924 season but also at the news that Coach Meagher's old boss from Notre Dame, Knute Rockne, was going to head a coaching school that summer at St. Ed's. A preview of opponents arrayed against the Saints revealed a tough schedule. Burleson (closed), named after the second president of Baylor and champions of the Junior College Conference the previous season, would also be a tough matchup. Other strong challengers included Louisiana Poly, known "to give their opponents a hard tussle,"[27] and Baylor, expected champions of the Southwest Conference.

The 1924 football season saw another successful team in St. Ed's. School spirit was noted during the Louisiana Poly and Tulsa games with a decent-sized student body in attendance, including three teammates who were injured. Pep rallies before the games set the stage, but the biggest by far was the Baylor pep rally, the biggest game of the season. The first game against the North Texas Agricultural College Aggies (now University of Texas–Arlington) was a shutout, 13–0, with Aillet coming off the bench to make a touchdown pass to teammate Williams. Aillet got some playing time in the victory over Schreiner Institute (now Schreiner University). While en route to another shutout (20–0), this time against the Southwest State Teacher's College (now Texas State), Aillet threw for the second touchdown of the day with a pass to Marvin "Mibbs" Durrenberger.

Other games where the opponent did score were often in the last moments of the game, when the reserves of the Saints were playing. One such instance was against a team from Louisiana Poly. In that game, the Saints' running game was too much, as the final score was 28–12.[28] Playing for Poly was George "Blue" Hogg. Shortly before the game, an accident occurred. The Bulldogs were riding in by rail when a railway bridge burned. The team wired ahead, requesting a few minutes' respite from the start time, but St. Edward's insisted on starting on time. The Bulldogs geared up on the train and barely made it in on time. Poly players began dropping out over the game's duration due to exhaustion. Hogg, a fullback, quickly found himself playing every position possible in the defeat to the St. Edians. Incidentally, Hogg, a future Bulldog coach with Aillet, graduated from Haynesville High School in 1922, a decade before Aillet's leadership of the Golden Tornado.[29]

The Golden Hurricane of Tulsa would not gain revenge from last season, as the Saints beat them with a the same score from the previous year, 35–7.

Between the two quarterbacks, O'Connor and Aillet, every play run seemed to be the correct call. In that game, Aillet hit Durrenberger again with a 25-yard touchdown pass in his first series as quarterback in the game to cap off a very active drive. Also playing a dominant game was the Saints line both ways. That was the last game Tulsa played against St. Ed's to date.[30] St. Ed's dropped football during World War II and never restarted the program.

The Baylor game, however, the first of two losses of the season, was a tough defeat. At the time the game was played, Baylor was the Southwest Conference champions. Despite having a better statistical game and gaining more first downs than the opponent, St. Ed's did not win. St. Ed's 172 yards of passing was more than the entire Baylor team's offensive production. Again, the line played forcefully. In the end, costly penalties (occurring at times beneficial to Baylor), turnovers and injuries were the deciding factors. What looked like an early touchdown pass from Thorny O'Connor to Lee "Ding" Meredith, coming back from an injured shoulder, was not to be; Meredith juggled the ball, and it was ruled incomplete. Most notably, triple-threat back Moose Woeber, one of the best and most consistent players on the team, received a season-ending knee injury in the first quarter, devastating team morale.[31]

Christmas Day saw another meeting of football greats. Coach Meagher, Father James Quinlan and Father Mooney visited with the Notre Dame football team at Houston. Before arriving in Houston, Rockne and the Notre Dame team had visited Aillet's alma mater, Holy Cross School in New Orleans.[32] Undefeated Notre Dame and the immortal Four Horsemen had an upcoming date with Stanford in the Rose Bowl. Rockne and Notre Dame would go on to defeat Pop Warner's Stanford, 27–10, ending the season with a 10-0 record and first national championship in school history.

Praise for Aillet was not sparing in recognition of his football performance in the '24 season: "Joe has all the good qualities of a quarterback. He has the knack of getting the best out of a team."[33] Although the team did not repeat an undefeated season, Aillet and his teammates were acknowledged for their efforts. The new year, 1925, brought an evolution in St. Edward's athletics. The Saints became a member of the Texas Interscholastic Athletic Association. It would be four years, however, before they could be full members. The college also became recognized as a senior college, or rather a university with the four-year requirements of a bachelor's degree, and member of the Association of Texas Colleges.

The 1925 basketball season looked to be up in the air. Several players were injured from football, such as Moose Woeber, and others were not

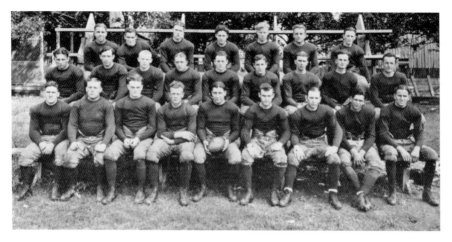

The 1923 St. Edward's football team. Aillet is first from left on top row. *From the* St. Edward's Tower, *1924.*

available; John Niemic, a star athlete of the college and baseball captain, had transferred to Notre Dame, and Stuessy was back home when he received news of the death of his brother.[34]

Indeed, the start to the basketball season took a toll, especially considering that most of their games were on the road. Lack of team cohesion was evident in the loss of the first game. Although Aillet and teammate James Vignos made a potent scoring duo, their early success could not be sustained. With defense lacking, there was little that could be done against San Marcos (now Southwest Texas State), losing 31–17.[35]

In a 29–13 victory over Austin College, Aillet led the team in scoring with 12 points. Aillet again was the team leader in scoring at the first game of a back-to-back with Simmons, netting 9 points. Unlike the previous smooth encounter, the Simmons game was far more physical but still a victory for St. Ed's. The next game against Simmons was also a victory, nearly a repeat in physicality and the final score.[36]

The closest game of a four-game road trip came against Abilene Christian College (now Abilene Christian University) in which the Saints lost, 33–29, despite scoring being spread among the team. Adding insult to injury, Moose Woeber received another knee injury, rendering him unavailable for the final road contest. In a similarly close match, St. Ed's fell to McMurry University, although Aillet once again led the team in scoring with 12 points.

The second game against Southwest Texas State was more successful, as a team effort brought forth a crushing victory, 31–18, thanks in part to high scoring from Aillet and good team defense.

The first game against Stephen F. Austin Teacher's College ended in tragedy. Moose Woeber, for the first time since the Abilene Christian game, was able to play. However, he was out in the second half, as his knee became aggravated again. Even though his performance greatly inspired the team, victory could not be had. To end the season on a good note, however, the final game was won against Stephen F. Austin. With Woeber well enough to play one last time, the team played inspired and won a convincing victory, 38–17.[37]

Thus was the basketball season wrapped up. Although numerous challenges could have been detrimental to any team, the "fighting Irish" or "St. Edians" made a commendable effort.

The upcoming baseball season was one of high hopes, but tempered by the fact that only four lettermen were returning. Despite the worries of inexperience and injuries, the baseball team performed well in the 1925 campaign.

Anticipation remained for the upcoming coaching school to be held on campus. Rockne and friend Walter E. Meanwell, fellow World War I veteran and successful basketball coach of Wisconsin, were going to oversee their respective sports in a meeting of players, coaches and athletic directors from across the South.

When it came time for the long-awaited football and basketball camp in the summer, Coach Meagher needed help. The St. Edward's backfield was asked to stay and help tend to the rooms where the guests would be staying. Hundreds of participants were in attendance, aside from large groups of Austinites and other spectators of the surrounding area. Lectures by Rockne took a few hours, with the rest of the morning spent on demonstrations. The August weather held out for the first week, as the location was billed as having a comfortable Gulf breeze. However, the second week became almost unbearably hot. Lasting two weeks, the St. Edians were hard at work, whether learning all that they could of the "Notre Dame Box" offense made famous by the Fighting Irish or taking care of facilities. At night, the team was to serve supper and clean up.[38] On more than one occasion, Aillet was cleaning up when Rockne and other coaches were discussing events of the day and other matters. He swept and swept around the room, even when there was nothing left to sweep, so he could listen. Sometimes, the conversation died down. Later, he'd come back and sweep some more when it picked back up.[39]

What was to be a promising 1925 football season soon turned sour. Aillet was injured in a scrimmage and never got back to his former self in competition. He did make a touchdown in a game against the Tennessee Physicians of Memphis, 14–0, while playing as right end.[40] St. Ed's began playing home games at Texas's Memorial Stadium.[41] At the end of the season, captain John "Sod" Ryan made an Austin sportswriter's best right tackle, Durrenberger made best right end and Meagher was put in the same league as Dana X. Bible of Texas A&M as best coaches of the state. It was another successful conclusion for Meagher, his fourth winning season at St. Ed's. Aillet was a part of three of the four. Also, despite his limited capacity, Aillet still managed to letter his last year of playing football.

It is unclear why Joe Aillet transferred to the University of Southwestern Louisiana Institute after finishing the first semester of his junior year at St. Ed's. Shortly before his departure, it appeared as if he was expected to play basketball. In fact, he was listed on the staff for the January 1926 edition of the *Echo*. For the first time, Aillet attended a nonreligious school, as well as one that was coeducational.

Certainly, Joe Aillet served his school well. Although he left St. Edward's, he made the school's football all-time roster and the basketball all-time roster.

CHAPTER 4

BACK HOME

While we don't know why he left St. Edward's for Southwestern, it did mean that he was closer to familiar surroundings, including his family and his sweetheart, Ruby Comeaux. During his time there, however, he was just as involved as he had been at St. Edward's. He became the governor and representative on the Inter-Fraternity Council of Sigma Pi Alpha, served on the committee for the Senior Ball, was a member of the Commercial Club, played golf and served as a student coach for football, baseball and basketball. Aillet was one of three boys voted by students in the categories of most popular, most intelligent and most representative, essential qualities in the making of a football coach.[42]

Aillet did not play football his senior year. Nevertheless, he contributed to the Bulldogs' winning season. The 1926 season saw several underclassmen on the team compared to the fourteen seniors of the previous season. In fact, it had been future New York Giant and College football Hall of Famer Christian "Red" Cagle's last year playing at Southwestern. It would therefore be no small feat in preparing the team for a new season under Head Coach T.R. Mobley; Aillet would have been assisting him and gaining experience. Indeed, Coach Mobley had overseen several good teams at Southwestern in recent years.

While not having as successful a season as the previous two-loss season, the Bulldogs still managed a 6-3-1 season. Most of the games were high-scoring and lop-sided on the scoreboard. The Bulldogs won shutouts against Sam Houston State, Austin College and South Park College, while losing

Left: Joe Aillet, student at Southwestern. *From Cynthia Aillet Murry.*

Right: Ruby Comeaux in college. *From Cynthia Aillet Murry.*

shutouts to LSU, Millsaps and the battle of the dogs with Louisiana Poly. Dominant shows were put on against Louisiana College and Louisiana Normal (now Northwestern State), a strong foe battled to a scoreless tie. The final matchup of the season was the Thanksgiving game against Mississippi College, which saw a thoroughly entertaining come-from-behind victory for the Bulldogs (20–16).[43] Games were well attended by the student body and people of Lafayette, making for an enthusiastic home crowd. The timely Sam Houston State victory was the first on the new athletic field of the school, occurring on the same day that former governor Henry Fuqua was honored after his passing.[44] It was the first time, however, that Southwestern lost on their new field when Poly later beat them.[45]

Students, faculty and alumni of the University of Louisiana, Lafayette and Louisiana Tech may be curious about the mascot of Southwestern. The Bulldogs remained the school mascot from 1921 until 1963, when they became the "Ragin' Cajuns."[46] The Louisiana Tech Bulldog traces back to 1899, five years after the founding of the university.[47]

Among Southwestern's greatest rivals is, in fact, Louisiana Poly. The 1926 matchup was the ninth of a series going back to 1910. The first game was a whopping 75–0 Poly victory, though in recent years, Southwestern proved to have the edge. The game attracted special attention, as a popular slogan was "Beat Polytech or bust." Southwestern's loss evened the series with Poly to 4-4, as the second game in the series had been a tie.

Although Aillet spent time assisting the coaching staff for basketball and baseball, those were not to be his future sport. At the same time, his experience playing those sports undoubtedly made some contribution to the teams those seasons. These teams were not successful in their 1927 seasons but showed promise among their underclassmen.

By the end of Aillet's final year of college at Southwestern, he had experienced two profound and life-altering moments. Not only did he graduate from Southwestern—majoring in history, commerce, English and mathematics[48]—but he also married Ruby Comeaux. Ruby had much in common with Joe. Both attended Southwestern, both were athletes, both were good dancers, both were Cajun, both were from Youngsville and both were raised to be strong Catholics. They would also become teachers, Ruby teaching briefly at Mamou High School. Coach Aillet's teaching brought him to North Louisiana.[49] It was the beginning of a happy life together.

CHAPTER 5

COACHING THE GOLDEN TOR

Upon graduation from Southwestern, Joe Aillet began what would be his lifelong profession in coaching football. Beginning on the high school level as an assistant, he took a job at a location which was unlike anything he had ever experienced.

Haynesville is a small town in northwest Louisiana, close to the Arkansas line. Instead of flat, marshy land and Gulf breezes, there existed rolling hills of red clay and towering pines swaying in the wind. Very few if any Catholics were to be found in this part of the Bible Belt. In fact, Coach Aillet later commented to Louisiana Poly player and dear friend A.L. Williams that he thought he would be the only Catholic in town. "I was wrong," he said, "There was one more!"—his wife. Also, very few if any Cajuns or Francophones were to be found. Indeed, perhaps the only commonalities between the two would be an abundance of oil and passion for football.

When A.L. Williams, who grew up in Haynesville, asked him three decades later what made him want to go to Haynesville, Coach Aillet fully understood the young man's curiosity. He could have easily taken a job in South Louisiana, especially at a Catholic school. Having played at Holy Cross, he could have coached in the Catholic League in New Orleans, widely seen as the best area in the state to coach football. Coach Aillet answered that it was the best coaching job in high school in the state of Louisiana at that time. When asked what made it the best, he said, "What those people in Haynesville wanted were two things: a good education for their children and good football. And if you could give them that, they would do anything they could to help you. It was a pleasant place to coach."[50]

Coach Aillet's journey to Haynesville could be considered an accident, coincidence or perhaps an invisible, guiding hand. Pat Rogers, principal of Homer, the nearby rivals of Haynesville, was teaching at Southwestern in the summer after Aillet's graduation. Haynesville principal Joe Farrar, who would become a valuable friend to Aillet, accepted Rogers's recommendation without even bothering with a personal interview. As Coach Aillet told Williams later, "It put me in a town more dedicated to its football than any other geographic area I know. People lived and died with the football operation."

Football was not the end to the means, however, for the Golden Tornado:

> *Football was a tradition in Claiborne Parish. The people believed a great deal about the education system and athletics and gave their total support to their facilities. The boys were oriented toward football, most being reared on farms or working in the oilfields and were very strong physically. I can't say enough about the type of people in Haynesville. They have so much confidence in their school system and athletics and above all, wanted their kids to get an education.[51]*

At the time he rode up to his new home with his new wife, however, Coach Aillet was not sure of his decision. He had entered a foreign world, though not completely foreign. They spoke the language of football very fluently. Haynesville football has been known, from the first team to take the field in 1907, as a state powerhouse. The Golden Tornado, or Golden Tor, originally the Golden Streak, was coached by Jess Hair. Hair, a graduate of Louisiana Poly, was most likely one of Aillet's earliest personal connections to the school where he would spend most of his coaching career.

Aillet was an assistant coach from 1927 to 1930 before becoming the head coach from 1931 to 1935, in addition to teaching at different times commerce, civics, history and arithmetic. Aillet would also find himself coaching other sports, as it was common at that time for coaches to coach multiple sports. During these years, Haynesville built on previous years' successes. Coach Hair was an assistant on the 1924 Haynesville team for Coach John H. Hendricks, the first in school history to win the state title. After that, Haynesville had several winning seasons.

At the end of April 1931, it was revealed that Coach Hair would coach at Biloxi, leaving behind a successful program, including the 1929 state championship. Aillet's new assistant coach was Cecil Crowley, a recent graduate of Centenary College who would later prove himself as a capable head coach.

The budding state powerhouse was bolstered by a passionate fan base. Local interest was such that they kept up with team activity at any cost. For example, the one road victory in Coach Aillet's first year at Haynesville, 1927, came against Winnfield. Fans at the game sent telegram updates to everyone back home, the last message relaying the 7–6 conclusion in favor of Haynesville.[52] The school gained a new field in 1928. Enthusiastic fans spilled out and watched games from the fence; when hedges were planted to deter this, fans would watch from nearby rooftops.[53] Coach Aillet thrived in this kind of environment.

On occasion, fans wanted to learn more about the game. In 1929, Aillet penned a brief article in the *Haynesville News* on the rules of football, as many locals wished to better keep track of the games. An action by the Ruston team stirred fans' curiosity, as a complaint was made to the umpire that one of the Bearcat players was not wearing a jersey, which was against the rules. He was made to put his jersey on. Aillet included an old story about how standard game balls were agreed upon. The Carlisle Indians, a school that was made up entirely of Native Americans and coached by the legendary Glenn "Pop" Warner, wore leather strips in the shape and color of a football on their uniforms to confuse the Harvard Crimson as to who had the ball. When the game began, however, Harvard provided crimson-colored footballs, matching their jerseys. Carlisle agreed to play with regular-colored leather balls once they tore off their jersey distractions. Umpires should make sure balls have proper dimension, air pressure and weight, and the referee should carry a pressure gauge, weights and scales to make this determination (although they rarely do).[54] One could only imagine what Coach Aillet would have to say about the NFL's Deflategate!

Always one for improving the infrastructure of athletic facilities, Coach Aillet had the charging machine, tackling dummy and scoreboard rebuilt in 1933.[55] In what would be a move unheard of today, Coach Aillet offered to demonstrate Golden Tor plays to the public in the beginning of the '33 season. Anyone who was interested could come to the gym and watch demonstrations—even Homer fans were invited! No one today would think of attempting such an event, as playbooks are some of the most closely guarded secrets of teams and coaches. As a matter of fact, several coaches in the modern era host secluded practices and bar members of the public from watching. Not so with Coach Aillet. This was for the benefit of the fans to better understand what was happening on the field.[56] Before the first game of 1934, Coach Aillet hosted a meeting for fans where he demonstrated the team playbook and what to expect from opponents through lectures and team demonstrations.

As there were no classifications other than "A" and "B" schools at this time, small "A" schools like Haynesville frequently played against giants like Byrd High School of Shreveport. This did not discourage the community; in fact, they reveled in the opportunity as a David to take down Goliath. Coach Aillet would embrace such a role in his coaching career.

Coach Aillet gained a reputation for meticulously preparing for each season. Overseeing spring training since 1929, he was widely known to carry a clipboard of timed drills for practice. Football practice was tough, as could be expected; Crowley took care of the line, and Aillet took care of the backfield. It would appear to be a tough first season, as the new team was absent several experienced players in both the line and backfield. As usual, the Haynesville team was undersized compared to several competitors.

Coach Aillet attended football camps and encouraged others to do so as well. While Coach Aillet worked with the boys at home, Coach Hair attended the two-week Knute Rockne coaching camp held at SMU in 1929.[57] No doubt he became familiar with much of what Coach Aillet had learned from Rockne over the years. In July 1932, Coach Aillet attended a coaches' camp in Lubbock, Texas. Several big names of the time were there, including his old coach at St. Edward's, Jack Meagher, then head coach of Rice Institute (now Rice University).[58]

In one example of the Byrd-Haynesville crusades, the Byrd Yellowjackets and Golden Tor remained on a collision course in the '33 postseason. Both teams had tied 6-6 in the regular season. In a playoff committee, it was determined that a three-way playoff would be held between Bossier City High School, Byrd and Haynesville. Bossier City claimed the district championship as having an undefeated record, including no ties, and having no points scored against them at any point in the season. Principal Farrar as chairman, however, decided that Bossier City did not have a championship-caliber schedule like Byrd and Haynesville. Thus, the committee—made up of Farrar, Grover Koffman of Byrd and S.M. Brown of Alexandria High School—settled on the three-way playoff. The teams that tied each other drew lots for who would play Bossier City, with Byrd's name being drawn.[59]

Games in different sports were frequently played against Arkansas schools. Athletes included the likes of Paul "Bear" Bryant and Lynwood "Schoolboy" Rowe. Haynesville played a postseason football game in 1927 against Fordyce, Arkansas, at Magnolia A&M (now Southern Arkansas University) football field. A precursor to an all-state versus all-state game, the encounter resulted in a 26–6 loss for the Golden Tor.[60] The Fordyce team had a freshman, Paul Bryant, who would have a bright future in the sport.

A final game of the 1934 season was arranged between Lafayette and Haynesville for Thanksgiving Day. Independent of the playoffs, it still produced a playoff-like atmosphere. Haynesville locals spent many days leading up to the contest trying to pronounce the names of the Cajuns making up the roster, undoubtedly helped by Aillet when possible, although he might have eventually given up on the endeavor. Some rumors persisted that they spoke French on the playing field to confuse opponents; it was also said that the game official at Neville made them stop speaking French because he could tell by the looks on their faces that they were insulting the opposing team. Coached by Louis "Louey" Whitman, a former Homer and Louisiana Poly football player, the dynamics of a southern team coached by a northerner versus a northern team coached by a southerner surely must have made for an entertaining advertisement.[61] It was the first game in Haynesville history devoted to a coach; due to Aillet's connections to Lafayette, the players especially wanted to win the game for him.[62]

Coach Aillet was involved with some of the most well-behaved football teams. The Majestic Hotel sent a handwritten note congratulating the 1929 team and said that theirs was, with one exception being the Baton Rouge team they hosted twice that season, the nicest, best-behaved and most gentlemanly team ever entertained at the hotel. The parents of the athletes were also commended as they concluded, "It would be a great day for the hotels of the general public and for the good name of the great name of football if they would follow the example set by your splendid team."[63] The acknowledgements, according to the *Haynesville News*, "showed that in developing a winning team the coaches had also developed gentlemen as well."[64]

Haynesville also received a congratulations on the conduct of the 1933 team from hotel management at Pine Bluff: "Of all the teams that we ever had with us, your boys were the most well behaved, most considerate, and most likeable bunch it has ever been our pleasure to have. We enjoyed having them with us and we hope they return real soon…for they were a bunch of real gentlemen."[65]

As Aillet's time at Haynesville concluded, Crowley, in his new position as head coach, received Bertis Yates, who returned to his hometown as assistant coach from an incredible four years playing LSU football. Aillet was leaving the school in good hands, as both would prove to be championship-caliber head coaches. Before his departure, he was designated honorary mayor of Haynesville, having so inspired the outstanding citizens of the town not just with his successful coaching but also with his mentorship of the youth and his unique personality.[66] His last act at Haynesville was gifting the school with fifteen black-and-gold plaques for the first fifteen football seasons with the names of lettermen for each respective season engraved. These included the first lettermen up to those of the present season.[67] He wished to establish it as a tradition to honor the lettermen.

Throughout Aillet's head coaching career at Haynesville, several of his players became All-Staters and college players. This was nothing new to Haynesville, which had a proud history before Aillet, but he contributed greatly to it. Several of his players became team captains in college and had successful careers. Joseph T. "Rock" Reed, for example, became team captain at LSU and helped the Tigers win their first SEC Championships, as well as making LSU's first two Sugar Bowls, one in 1935 and one in 1936 while Aillet was at Louisiana Normal. After college, he would become the first Haynesville football player to play professional football, playing for the Chicago Cardinals.[68] Later, in 1947, Coach Aillet faced his former player as a coach for an opposing team. Reed, while completing studies at Southwestern, coached the backfield of the South Louisiana Bulldogs. The Rustonians won 9–0. Ironically, Coach Aillet wore a red victory tie given to him by Reed while at Haynesville to wear when his team won a game.[69]

While Aillet's record at Louisiana Tech rightfully distinguishes his career as a football coach, his record at Haynesville stands as one of the best, not just for the school but for the state. At no point did Aillet register a losing season, and at no point did the team lose more than two games in a season. From 1931 to 1935, Haynesville recorded 33 wins, 7 losses, and 5 ties, a 79 percent win percentage and the fourth-highest win percentage of any coach at Haynesville.[70] And while Aillet's tenure of five seasons ranks fifth longest for a Haynesville football coach, he accomplished much in those seasons. He could have remained in the high school ranks at Haynesville and built on his successes. His teams scored 950 total points, while having 151 total points scored against them. This averages to 190 points scored on average per season, while having 30.2 points scored against them on average per season. Most of these points were surrendered to rivals Homer and Byrd, primarily Byrd. Although he never beat Byrd, the team to beat of the 1930s, Aillet did tie against them three times. Against Homer, he won three, lost one and tied one. In fact, these were the only teams in Louisiana, except for Lake Charles in the 1932 state championship game, to beat him. His record against out-of-state schools was 5-1-1; Pine Bluff was the only out-of-state school to beat him, while four of five victories were shutouts. In playoff games, he was 0-2. If he had chosen to remain at Haynesville, he had a very good chance to make it back to the state championship and win. Of course, if that happened, there could have never been the Tech connection that has defined his life and memory.

Many memories were made at Haynesville, in football and in other ways. Two of the Aillet children were born while the family resided in Haynesville. The first to be welcomed by Joe and Ruby, Bobby, came in early 1928. Just as the 1931 season was about to get underway, Cynthia was born.

Aillet proved early on to be innovative and adaptive. Bringing in his prior knowledge from Southwestern and all those developmental years spent with schools run by the Congregation of Holy Cross, he kept the competitive spirit alive at Haynesville. Aillet was well respected; his calm demeanor, fairness and careful explanation of football won him many admirers. The caliber of athletes produced by Haynesville also points to the early mentorship qualities he would display in the future. In fact, one of his final acts before leaving Haynesville involved hosting veterans of the First World War to speak at his history classes. As a leader, he helped establish the North Louisiana High School Coaches' Association; in 1935, his last year, he established the Louisiana High School Coaches' Association and served as the first president.[71] Last but not least, the singing spirit developed as a youth never left him, as he frequently sang at social events in town. He would indeed be missed for his contributions to the school and community.

CHAPTER 6

NEW JOB, ANOTHER UNDEFEATED SEASON

A t the conclusion of 1935, Joe Aillet would find himself returning to the college ranks as the first assistant football coach at Louisiana Normal and assistant professor of physical education. Located in the town of Natchitoches, it retained a strong historic and cultural French Colonial heritage. While there were some Haynesville players on previous Louisiana Normal rosters, Aillet's presence likely contributed to future Demon teams being dominated by graduates of the Golden Tor. He would assist Coach Harry "Rags" Turpin, so named because of his flamboyant wardrobe.[72]

While rivalries with Louisiana Poly and Southwestern were keenly observed, several opponents were led by star players of the mid- to late '30s. The Mississippi State Teachers, or Southern Miss, were led by standout Leo Purvis, the uncle of future Southern Miss star Vic Purvis, in 1936. The 1938 Centenary team was led by All-SIAA (Southern Intercollegiate Athletic Association) back and future New York Giant Weenie Bynum; East Texas was led by All-American tailback and future Detroit Lion Darrell Dean Tully, and All-SIAA halfback Glynn Abel led Southwestern.

Rags Turpin, a former athlete of Normal, was in his third year as head coach. It was a tough season, as the team went 5-4-1, but it was an improvement from the previous season's 2-9 record. In the 1936 homecoming loss to East Texas, sustaining gruesome injuries even with a stalwart defense, the Demon offense often lacked the punch needed to score.[73] Similar problems from previous years plagued the team. While an assistant coach at Haynesville, Aillet coached the backfield; he would distinguish himself for his coaching the backfield at Normal, a fitting area for a former quarterback.

The year 1937 proved to be a very similar year as '36. Again, injuries and an inconsistent offense, despite a fearsome defense, proved to be the culprit of many a defeat. For example, after tying the season opener against Centenary College, a very beat-up Demon team lacking eleven starters was crushed on the road only three days later against East Texas. The game scheduled against Magnolia A&M had to be canceled, with so many injuries over the last two games played so close in succession.[74] The year 1937 was also the first of six-man football among small colleges, an innovation credited to Coach Aillet.[75]

During the 225th anniversary of the town of Natchitoches, Louisiana Normal broke even again. While injuries persisted in robbing the Demons of much-needed players, the offense improved. Mistakes such as fumbles and inconsistent punting, however, persisted. The season began with three straight losses.

Statistically, 1938 would point to an encouraging future. Louisiana Normal scored 97 total points, outscoring opponents by 17 in total points. A friendly visit by national champions TCU, the victors of the Sugar Bowl over Carnegie Tech, as well as a visit by Lowell "Red" Dawson, head coach of Tulane, at the annual football banquet topped off a roller coaster season for the Demons.[76] With the university adding several new structures on campus, Louisiana Normal was experiencing a period of rapid growth. The Aillet family also experienced growth with the birth of their third child and second son, Richard "Dickie" Aillet.

It is no doubt that Aillet quickly found himself at home at Louisiana Normal. Aside from the Cajun-speaking population, he and Ruby had the opportunity to send their children to St. Mary's for a Catholic education.[77] The summer of '37 saw Coach Turpin attend LSU for his master's and Dr. C.C. Stroud of the athletic department visit Boston hospitals and attend lectures at Boston University, leaving the summer responsibilities of athletic courses to Aillet.[78] He became an honorary member of the "N" Club, celebrating those who lettered in a sport at Normal, and became one of a small group of faculty, including H.L. Prather—basketball coach, athletic director and dean of men—who were honorary "N" Club members.

The year 1939 saw the fruition of years of hard work. Many players graduated the previous year, including captain and All-SIAA guard Walter Ledet, the first All-American in Louisiana Normal history; Ledet was also renowned for his kicking ability, kicking extra points that decisively beat Sam Houston, 7–6, in 1936 and Louisiana Poly, 7–6, in 1938, as well as the field goal that beat the Mississippi Teachers, 3–0, in 1937.[79] The Demons made more history by securing their first undefeated season. They were, for the first time in school history, the only undefeated and untied team in the state and champions of the SIAA and Louisiana Intercollegiate Conference.[80] It was accomplished in dominant fashion, as total points scored by opponents were only 18 to the 195 of the purple and white, from Centenary to East Texas, Southeastern, Mississippi Delta, Stephen F. Austin, Louisiana College, Louisiana Poly, Mississippi State Teachers, Southwestern and others, including Murray Teachers (now Murray State University) and Ouachita College, coached by Bill Walton, formerly an Arkansas high school football coach whom Aillet faced off against while coaching at Haynesville. The Gents were defeated by Louisiana Normal for the first time since play between the two schools began in 1921.[81]

Discussion of a bowl game fell through. Over the Christmas holiday, several faculty and students of Louisiana Normal had severe accidents, including Coach Turpin, who fainted at the Sugar Bowl game and received a gash above his right eye after falling on the bleachers.[82] The big game appeared to be bad luck, when taking into account the Louisiana Poly coaches' car accident returning from the Sugar Bowl two years prior. Coach Aillet was about to turn a significant page in his life and career, one that would make a definitive statement in Louisiana sports history and at a college that he had long been destined for over the years. Rumors were shot down toward the end of the season that he would leave to coach at Rice;[83] instead, the road led north. During his time at Normal, the team was 25-13-2. Now he would look to leave his mark as a head football and golf coach, a sport he was slated to take over at Normal before leaving.

CHAPTER 7

ANOTHER NEW JOB, BUILDING A CHURCH

When Joe Aillet came to Ruston, Louisiana, in 1940, he would have found it similar in some respect to Haynesville. Ruston was like many small towns in the piney hills Bible Belt of North Louisiana. What made Ruston stand out, however, was its center of higher education. Louisiana Polytech had prestige and drew many businesses, religious groups and people involved in sports to the college town.

When Aillet arrived, no Catholic church existed in Ruston. Any Catholics who did live in the area were primarily Poly students and family members. The campus Newman Club, founded the previous year, held its first meetings in the house of Poly student Anne Bleich. The international organization is for Catholic students at secular postsecondary institutions. Other meeting locations were the McLane house, as Poly football coach Eddie McLane's wife and daughter were Catholic, and the Aillet house. Priests occasionally came from neighboring Monroe; Masses were celebrated at the Education Building. When a priest was not present on Sundays, the Aillets simply knelt in their living room and Ruby led them in prayers. Such minimalism was less than ideal.

Of the small group of eight to twelve Catholic families who lived in Ruston at the time, several were Cajun. They were a welcome group of companions for the Aillets. Aside from sharing the same faith, they spoke the same language. Occasionally, they would host a language evening where everyone would gather to socialize, speaking only Cajun French.

However, Joe and Ruby wanted their children to learn English and speak only English. At the time, Cajun French was discouraged in Louisiana, and students were punished in schools for speaking it. When speaking on the phone to relatives in Youngsville, if a topic came up that Ruby didn't want the children to know about, she would speak in French. This was not so helpful, for as they got older, Bobby and Cynthia picked up enough of the language to be able to understand what was being said. Finally, Joe and Ruby began using the language less and less. Relatives were told not to encourage or use French in front of the kids. Bobby and Cynthia's grandmother would ask them what she just said, and they would correctly repeat it in English. One day, Cynthia was going down the street in front of her grandmother's house and met a close family friend. As she was skipping, hopping and jumping along, she said "good morning" in French. "What did you say? I'm going to tell your grandmother you're learning to speak French!" Incidents like that were embarrassing enough to get her to refrain from being too vocal about her knowledge of the language.

The fact that a church did not exist in the growing city greatly troubled Coach Aillet. "These youngsters need a place to go to Mass. They have to have that."[84] Much to his and other Catholics' relief, their religious needs would soon be served by the construction of a church.

Education Building on Louisiana Tech campus. *From* The Lagniappe, *1940.*

The timing was opportune in several respects. During the previous football season, the Newman Club chapter was established at Louisiana Poly. This is significant given the geographic and cultural underpinnings of the university. Nevertheless, progress had been made by the small but dedicated number of Catholics in the area. The forty Newman Club members of Normal attended an inauguration banquet at Poly along with the thirty new Tech members, President Edwin Richardson of Poly and the sponsors and chaplains for both schools: Father Aycock of Normal and Father Donahue of Poly.[85] These two priests were among the original priests from St. Matthew's Catholic Church in Monroe who celebrated Mass in Ruston in the years leading up to the establishment of the Newman Club.

Father Henry Freiburg was the first Franciscan priest of the area. His efforts helped spearhead the movement for a church in Ruston. "Those students, who are leaders of tomorrow in many fields of endeavor, should be thoroughly grounded in the principles of the Christian faith,"[86] stated Father Freiburg in a circular letter sent to Catholics across the state. Local businessman J.H. Campbell also had a key role in raising funds. "We have long felt that the presence of so many Catholic students on the Tech campus justified the building of a church."[87]

When St. Paschal's Catholic Church of West Monroe was completed in 1940, Father Freiburg became its pastor. He was succeeded in Ruston by Father Jasper Mauss. Upon completion of the new church in Ruston, Father Mauss became the first priest to celebrate Mass on April 20, 1941. Dedication was conducted by Bishop Daniel F. Desmond of Alexandria on December 14.[88] The church would be dedicated to St. Thomas Aquinas, a medieval scholastic, doctor of the church and patron of all universities, academies, colleges and schools. The original bell, which still exists outside the current church building, was donated by Dr. George Poret, a professor of psychology at Poly. The bell came from his grandfather Isidore Poret's plantation in Avoyelles Parish. After purchasing the bell from an individual who bought it at an auction in 1878, Poret donated it to the new church. The altar was also noted for its beauty.[89] An early addition to the church was the beginning of a library by the Ladies Altar Society; both the library and the LAS continue to this day.[90]

World War II occupied the attention of the ministers of St. Thomas Aquinas and Coach Aillet. Father Humilius Soland became the first pastor of the church. Camp Ruston, a World War II prison camp that would have a profound impact on Ruston, needed religious ministers. Father Humilius contributed his services to the cause.[91] One major event that took place at

Original St. Thomas Aquinas Catholic Church. *From St. Thomas Aquinas Catholic Church, Ruston, Louisiana.*

Side view of St. Thomas Aquinas. *From St. Thomas Aquinas Catholic Church, Ruston, Louisiana.*

Bishop Charles Pascal Greco of the Diocese of Alexandria blessing the new Student Center. *From St. Thomas Aquinas Catholic Church, Ruston, Louisiana, 1968.*

St. Thomas Aquinas was the Memorial Day Celebration of 1943. After a well-attended Mass by servicemen, a street procession concluded with the dedication of the papal flag and the American flag.[92] When Father Humilius became a military chaplain in 1944, Father Myron Landolt became the second pastor of St. Thomas Aquinas and was followed by Father Eusebius Brezovsky in 1946, who stayed for two years as well.

The fourth pastor of St. Thomas Aquinas, Father Severin Nelles, founded a parochial school on church grounds. Completed in December 1951, the St. Thomas Aquinas School originally included kindergarten to fourth grade and would later be extended to eighth grade. The Franciscan Sisters of Our Lady of Perpetual Help of St. Louis, Missouri, operated the school.[93]

Joe Aillet speaking at the dedication of the Student Center. *From St. Thomas Aquinas Catholic Church, Ruston, Louisiana, 1968.*

St. Thomas Aquinas School was very important for the Aillets. Coach Aillet's grandchildren were educated there. It remained a small school and accepted non-Catholics as well. Sometimes this produced delicate yet humorous situations. Once, Ruby Aillet received a call from a next-door friend, whose son ran into the house insisting that some witches were chasing the Aillet kids. The "witches" turned out to be the sisters in their habits playing baseball with the kids. They held up their skirts while running the bases.[94]

The E. Donn Piatt Building, better known today as the Student Center and a landmark of St. Thomas Aquinas, was constructed in 1968 and named after the building contractor who donated for the construction of the building. Coach Aillet spoke highly of his character. Aillet also

Father Donnard Paulus with Newman Club students outside the Student Center. *From* The Lagniappe, *1968.*

acknowledged Father Donnard Paulus; Father Donnard first arrived at St. Thomas Aquinas in 1957, the same year Piatt died. It took several years for the idea to become a reality, including a temporary hold when Father Donnard left in 1963. Father Barnabus Diekemper served as the new pastor for a short time. Upon Donnard's return in 1966, the building was completed and provided a place for the Newman Club to gather.[95]

The Aillets had fond memories of St. Thomas Aquinas. Once, Father Donnard was walking down the front steps after Mass. Two of Cynthia's preschool children were there. "Look, Martha, it's Jesus," exclaimed Lisa. "That's not Jesus," corrected Martha, "That's God!" Father Donnard could only sit down on the steps laughing. Another time, Lisa was to crown the statue of the Blessed Mother in May Crowning. After crowning the Blessed Mother, she fainted while climbing down the ladder. Her older brother Mark, an altar boy, came to the rescue. After genuflecting when crossing the altar, he grabbed her heels and dragged her into the nearest room. Despite these incidents, Tech football graduates who came back to get married at the church requested their services at Mass.

Coach Aillet had been instrumental in the founding of St. Thomas Aquinas and remained devoted to it. He and other parishioners such as the Bleichs, Campbells, Porets and Piatts were heavily involved and formed a close-knit community. Coach Aillet's Catholic football players attended Mass at St. Thomas Aquinas. Ruby began what became a long-standing tradition of cooking a gumbo supper; originally meant as a fundraiser for church construction, it quickly became a community event.[96] The fulfilling experience of parish life, based on a strong foundation going back to his college days at St. Edward's and high school days at Holy Cross, undoubtedly sustained Coach Aillet through the ups and downs of life at Louisiana Poly. True to his faith, he remained concerned with not just winning but also providing mentorship for his athletes.

CHAPTER 8

ACCOMPLISHMENTS
AT LOUISIANA TECH

A proud tradition of Louisiana Tech Bulldog football existed before Joe Aillet became the twenty-second football coach of Tech. A few teams were formidable, but there had never developed long-term consistency. Only one other coach in Bulldog history is in the College Football Hall of Fame: William Henry "Lone Star" Dietz. Part of the story of Coach Aillet's success at Tech lies in the caliber of his players. Just as the teams could not have won without the star players, they also could not have won without the worthy contributions of other teammates.

Joe Michael made a selfless sacrifice in 1942. With World War II raging, he gave his team-signed football from the Southwestern game the previous season back to Tech in case it became difficult finding new footballs for play.[97]

The Bulldog scoring ability in 1949 was due to a fair amount of trickery not practiced in training sessions but rather improvised on the field; this is likely due to Jimmy Harrison's triple-threat athletic capabilities and an acuity by Bobby Aillet, who overruled his father on one occasion that led to a Bulldog touchdown at the State Fair.

Another Tech player proved a valuable codebreaker. A key observation by Joe Ross in the Wildcat route-running patterns allowed the Bulldogs to intercept three passes in the second half: one by himself, which iced the game in the final minute of play; one by Bud McMichael; and one by Gene Knecht, all with moderate returns in the 1951 victory, 20–14, over Louisiana College.[98]

TECH'S ALL-AMERICANS

| Ron Alexander | Charles Anderson | Terry Bradshaw | Gordon Brown | Tom Causey | Garland Gregory | Jerry Griffin |
| 1970 Linebacker | 1955 End | 1968-69 QB | 1952 End | 1960 End | 1941 Guard | 1961 End |

| Jimmy Harrison | Joe Hinton | Pat Hinton | Tommy Hinton | Jerry Hudson | Ken Lantrip | Russell Rainbolt |
| 1949 Halfback | 1959-60 Guard | 1956 Tackle | 1957 Tackle | 1959 End | 1971 QB | 1955 Halfback |

| Mike Reed | Chris Richardson | Mickey Slaughter | Ed Stassi | Jesse Storts | John R. Williamson | Johnny Wyss |
| 1946-47 Guard | 1971 Def. Guard | 1962 QB | 1948 Guard | 1954 Guard | 1963 Center | 1937 Guard |

TECH'S 1971 ALL-STARS

All-Southland Conference

FIRST TEAM OFFENSE

Pos.	Player, School	Wgt.	Hght.	Class
E	Steve Lockhart, Arkansas St.	230	6-3	Sr.
E	ERIC JOHNSON, La. Tech	165	5-8	Jr.
T	Bill Keresztury, Trinity Univ.	255	6-4	Jr.
T	Don Blair, Southwestern La.	214	6-1	Jr.
G	Wayne Dorton, Arkansas St.	248	6-2	Sr.
G	Louis Age, Southwestern La.	230	6-3	Sr.
QB	KEN LANTRIP, La. Tech	185	6-0	Sr.
RB	CHARLES McDANIEL, La. Tech	170	6-0	Fr.
RB	Calvin Harrell, Arkansas St.	223	6-1	Sr.
WR	Bill Hodge, Trinity Univ.	175	6-1	Jr.
C	PHIL ISRAEL, La. Tech	200	5-11	Sr.

FIRST TEAM DEFENSE

Pos.	Player, School	Wgt.	Hght.	Class
E	Steve Majka, Trinity Univ.	195	6-2	Jr.
E	Dave Muckensturm, Ark. St.	195	6-1	Jr.
T	FRED DEAN, La. Tech	212	6-4	Fr.
T	Gary Crockett, Lamar Univ.	222	6-4	Sr.
LB	Hiram Burleson, UT-Arlington	220	6-1	So.
LB	Bruce Jackson, Trinity Univ.	215	6-2	Sr.
LB	Verlon Murray, Ark. St.	218	6-1	Sr.
DB	Steve Ladislaw, Trinity Univ.	190	5-11	Jr.
DB	Patrick Gibbs, Lamar Univ.	185	6-0	Sr.
DB	Dennis Meyer, Ark. St.	195	5-11	Sr.
DB	Ernest Baptist, UT-Arlington	173	5-11	Jr.

Offensive Kicker, Joe Duren, Arkansas State
Defensive Kicker: MIKE SWINNEY, Louisiana Tech

All-Louisiana

OFFENSE

Tight End	James Moore	6-1	195	Jr.	McNeese
Wide Receiver	Andy Hamilton	6-3	190	Sr.	LSU
Wide Receiver	Steve Barrios	6-0	185	Sr.	Tulane
Running Back	Larry Grissom	6-1	206	Sr.	McNeese
Running Back	CHARLES McDANIEL	6-0	175	Fr.	La. Tech
Quarterback	KEN LANTRIP	6-0	185	Sr.	La. Tech
Center	Charles Powell	6-1	225	Sr.	McNeese
Guard	Solomon Freelon	6-4	256	Sr.	Grambling
Guard	Mike Demarie	5-10	220	Sr.	LSU
Tackle	Mike O'Quinn	6-3	225	Sr.	McNeese
Tackle	Charles Stuart	6-2	240	Sr.	LSU

DEFENSE

End	John Mendenhall	6-3	250	Sr.	Grambling
End	Mike Truax	6-3	195	So.	Tulane
Tackle	Ronnie Estay	6-1	225	Sr.	LSU
Tackle	Charles Allen	6-0	195	Sr.	McNeese
Middle Guard	CHRIS RICHARDSON	5-11	230	Sr.	La. Tech
Linebacker	Mike Mullen	6-2	230	Jr.	Tulane
Linebacker	Larry Rawlinson	6-1	210	Jr.	McNeese
Linebacker	Gordon Boogaerts	6-1	220	Jr.	Northwestern
Deep Back	Joe Bullard	6-0	185	Sr.	Tulane
Deep Back	Tommy Casanova	6-1	190	Sr.	LSU
Deep Back	Kerry Duplessis	5-11	185	Jr.	Southeastern

SPECIAL AWARDS

Coach of the Year	Jack Doland, McNeese
Offensive Lineman of the Year	Charles Powell, McNeese
Offensive Back of the Year	CHARLES McDANIEL, La. Tech
Defensive Lineman of the Year	Ronnie Estay, LSU
Defensive Back of the Year	Joe Bullard, Tulane

| Lantrip | McDaniel | Richardson | Johnson | Dean | Swinney | Israel |

The services of Charles Anderson, under ends coach Huey Williamson, were well appreciated. Before the Mississippi Southern game of '54, he was asked by the coaching staff if he would mind shifting from starting left end to being a second-string right end. Coach Aillet especially took note of this, that he "made a good example of team spirit by subduing any personal ambition for the benefit of the entire team."[99]

Seventy Years Of Football
1901 — Louisiana Tech — 1971

1901 (0-2-0)
Coach: Barber
Capt.: Unknown
0 Louisiana St. 57
0 U. of Ark. 16
0 (Rec. incom.) 73

1902 (?)
Coach: Frank Singleton
Capt.: Unknown
(Rec. unknown)

1903 (0-1-0)
Coach: Unknown
Capt.: Unknown
0 Louisiana St. 16
0 (Rec. incom.) 16

1904 (1-3-0)
Coach: E. G. Pierce
Capt.: Glenn M. Walker
0 Tulane U. 11
0 Louisiana St. 17
6 Louisiana St. 0
5 Miss. St. 32
11 60

1905 (0-1-0)
Coach: J. V. Bragg
Capt.: J. P. Pope
0 Louisiana St. 16
0 (Rec. incom.) 16

1906 (2-1-3)
Coach: Z. Y. Young
Capt.: H. T. Hair
0 Monroe Ath. 0
5 Oua. (Ar.) Col. 0
3 Louisiana St. 17
26 Ruston Ath. 0
5 Henderson-Brown Col. 5
0 YMCA Conf. 0
(S'port)
36 22

1907 (9-1-0)
Coach: George L. Watkins
Capt.: Dave Caldwell
11 Monroe Ath. Tm. 0
11 Monroe Ath. 0
0 Louisiana St. 28
37 Oua. (Ar.) Col. 0
43 La. St. Normal 0
21 Henderson-Brown 0
49 Ruston Ath. Tm. 0
35 Jackson Military Col. 0
23 Ark. College 5
18 Miss. College 0
248 37

1908 (4-3-1)
Coach: A. L. Cornell
Capt.: A. A. Smith
28 16th U.S. Infantry 0
--- Little Rock, Ar. ---
0 Miss. State 47
0 Centenary Col. 0
72 Hendrix (Ar.) Col. 0
10 Henderson-Brown Col. 0
18 16th U.S. Infnty. 6
77 Oua. (Ar.) Col. 0
0 Louisiana St. 22
205 91

1909 (4-1-0)
Coach: Percy S. Prince
Capt.: Walter Barr
28 Monroe Ath. 0
60 Centenary Col. 0
0 Louisiana St. 23
3 Henderson-Brown Col. 0
45 La. St. Normal 23
136

1910 (5-0-0)
Coach: Percy S. Prince
Capt.: Unknown
--- W. H. S. ---
0 Oua. (Ar.) Col. 0
--- Louisiana Col. ---
75 SW La. Institute 0
11 Henderson-Brown Col. 6
32 La. St. Normal 6
130 (Rec. incom.) 6

1911 (4-2-1)
Coach: Percy S. Prince
Capt.: A. A. Smith
0 U. of Miss. 15
6 Oua. (Ar.) Col. 0
5 Hendrix (Ar.) Col. 5
39 La. St. Normal 0
24 Miss. Col. 0
24 Henderson-Brown Col. 3

0 Tulane U. 45
98 68

1912 (0-2-1)
Coach: Percy S. Prince
Capt.: Unknown
0 Ouachita 0
13 Miss. Col. 14
0 Henderson St. 14
13 (Rec. incom.) 28

1913 (1-4-1)
Coach: Percy S. Prince
Capt.: Unknown
2 Louisiana St. 20
6 U. of Miss. 26
7 Centenary 0
0 Ouachita 0
0 Ouachita 19
3 Miss. Col. 14
12 79

1914 (0-2-0)
Coach: Percy S. Prince
Capt.: Unknown
0 Louisiana St. 60
0 Miss. Col. 46
0 (Rec. incom.) 106

1915 (2-1-2)
Coach: Percy S. Prince
Capt.: Unknown
20 La. St. Normal 7
7 SW La. Institute 7
0 Ouachita 19
0 Miss. Col. 0
43 Henderson St. 0
70 33

1916 (1-2-0)
Coach: Flack
Capt.: Unknown
0 SW La. Institute 26
0 Henderson St. 14
10 Ouachita 6
10 (Rec. incom.) 46

1917 (0-2-0)
Coach: V. S. Pugh
Capt.: Dewitt Milam
0 SW La. Institute 57
10 Ouachita 53
10 (Rec. incom.) 110

1918 — Football discontinued

1919 (0-1-1)
Coach: Percy S. Prince
Capt.: Unknown
7 Henderson St. 14
7 (Rec. incom.) 14

1920 (5-1-0)
Coach: R. F. Clark
Capt.: Bob Seegers
0 La. St. Normal 7
1 SW La. Institute (forfeit) 12
8 Magnolia A&M 0
13 St. Charles Col. 7
7 La. College 0
14 La. College 0
38 19

1921 (2-6-0)
Coach: R. F. Clark
Capt.: Roe Hollis
13 Ark. A&M 0
22 Magnolia A&M 13
20 Oua. (Ar.) Col. 0
20 SW La. Institute 0
15 La. St. Normal 0
14 Centenary Col. 7
104 20

1922 (5-1-1)
Coach: William H. Dietz
Capt.: Edgar L. Walker
33 Hendrix (Ar.) Col. 0
0 La. St. Normal 0
100 Clark Mem. Col. 0
34 Henderson-Brown Col. 0
33 Louisiana Col. 6
81 Magnolia A&M 0
0 Centenary Col. 20
281 26

1923 (2-7-1)
Coach: William H. Dietz
Capt.: Roe Hollis
26 Little Rock Col. 0
7 Henderson-Brown Col. 13
7 Tulane U. 13
20 Millsaps Col. 7
40 La. St. Normal 7
66 La. St. Normal 7
28 Loyola 7
27 Centenary Col. 27
194 63

1924 (1-6-1)
Coach: Phillip H. Arbuckle
Capt.: Otis Reed
0 Louisiana Col. 0
12 Tulane U. 42
0 U. of Dallas 9
12 Little Rock Col. 0
12 St. Edwards Col. 28
0 Oua. (Ar.) Col. 13
0 SW La. Institute 33
0 Loyola of South 27
42 139

1925 (1-6-2)
Coach: R. C. Kenney
Capt.: Unknown
0 Henderson-Brown Col. 0
6 Miss. Col. 0
6 Little Rock Col. 10
2 Millsaps Col. 13
0 Louisiana Col. 0
0 Oua. (Ar.) Col. 28
0 Tulane U. 37
13 SW La. Institute 22
7 Ft. Benning Infantry 66
28 176

1926 (5-2-2)
Coach: Hugh E. Wilson
Capt.: George B. Hogg
0 Tulane U. 40
28 La. St. Normal 0
36 Clark Mem. Col. 0
6 U. of Tenn. Dctrs. 0
13 Millsaps Col. 7
23 SW La. Institute 0
0 Centenary Col. 7
28 Louisiana Col. 0
6 Sam Houston St. 0
28 Louisiana Col. 0
134 60

1927 (3-5-0)
Coach: Hugh E. Wilson
Capt.: Harrell P. Willis
0 La. St. Normal 45
30 Clark Mem. Col. 0
0 Miss. St. 14
33 La. St. Normal 0
0 Miss. Col. 7
13 SW La. Institute 0
7 Stetson U. 19
0 Centenary Col. 33
83 118

1928 (2-7-0)
Coach: F. A. Rockwell
Capt.: Bill Slay
0 Col. of Ozarks 7
19 Clark Mem. Col. 6
0 La. St. Normal 52
0 Howard (Al.) Col. 52
0 Union (Tn.) U. 26
6 SW La. Institute 45
15 Millsaps Col. 7
2 Centenary Col. 63
0 Miss. Col. 12
42 235

1929 (4-4-2)
Coach: F. A. Rockwell
Capt.: Gale Burnham
21 Clark Mem. Col. 12
6 Magnolia A&M 7
13 Oua. (Ar.) Col. 0
0 La. St. Normal 53
0 Miss. Col. 21
0 Centenary Col. 19
13 Louisiana Col. 19
24 SW La. Institute 7
96 137

1930 (3-6-0)
Coach: George M. Bohler
Capt.: George Riser
0 Louisiana St. 71
0 Loyola of South 0
12 Ark. A&M 0
0 Miss. Col. 39
7 SW La. Institute 0
14 La. St. Normal 19
0 Millsaps 19
6 Centenary Col. 13
6 Louisiana Col. 7
39 187

1931 (7-0-0)
Coach: George M. Bohler
Capt.: W. Bennie Swyne
13 Copiah-Lncln. JC 7
39 Union (Tn.) U. 0
38 SW La. Institute 0
20 Millsaps Col. 7
18 La. St. Normal 7
19 Miss. Col. 13
27 Louisiana Col. 7
167 36

1932 (4-4-0)
Coach: George M. Bohler
Capt.: J. B. Durham
0 Copiah-Lncln. JC 2
46 Union (Tn.) U. 7
20 Delta St. Col. 0
0 SW La. Institute 33
19 Millsaps Col. 14
7 Miss. Col. 20
6 Louisiana Col. 13
113 89

1933 (1-7-0)
Coach: George M. Bohler
Capt.: Jimmy Davis
9 Copiah-Lncln. JC 10
0 Henderson St. Col. 7
19 SW La. Institute 13
10 Texas Tech 40
6 La. St. Normal 0
0 Col. of the Ozarks 40
0 Louisiana Col. 30
32 143

1934 (4-6-0)
Coach: L. P. "Eddie" McLane
Capt.: Ike Lowery
7 Holmes Jr. Col. 0
7 Magnolia A&M 0
0 Henderson St. Col. 27
0 SW La. Institute 25
41 Lambuth Col. 0
0 La. St. Normal 6
7 Millsaps Col. 13
0 Louisiana Col. 32
26 Delta St. Col. 13
0 Louisiana Col. 0
88 116

1935 (8-1-0)
Coach: L. P. "Eddie" McLane
Capt.: Madison Brooks
44 Tenn. Tech 0
25 SW La. Institute 0
27 Union (Tn.) U. 0
32 La. St. Normal 0
20 Millsaps Col. 21
25 Louisiana Col. 7
27 Miss. Sou. 0
32 U. of Tampa 7
253 47

1936 (6-2-1)
Coach: L. P. "Eddie" McLane
Capt.: Bennie L. Phillips
44 W. Tenn. Tchrs. 0
20 SW La. Institute 7
7 Miss. Sou. 12
32 La. St. Normal 0
22 U. of Tampa 0
13 Millsaps Col. 0
0 Louisiana Col. 0
12 Illinois Wesleyan 7
153 47

1937 (6-3-2)
Coach: L. P. "Eddie" McLane
Capt.: Johnny Wyss
27 Okla. City U. 0
0 U. of Miss. 13
0 Illinois Wesleyan 0
7 Millsaps Col. 0
0 Miss. Sou. 0
14 La. St. Normal 0
26 U. of Tampa 13
12 SW La. Institute 0
20 U. of S. Dakota 13
7 Centenary Col. 7
120 53

1938 (3-7-1)
Coach: L. P. "Eddie" McLane
Capt.: A. Huey Williamson
13 Miss. Col. 26
19 Millsaps Col. 7
7 U. of Miss. 20
0 Miss. St. 48
6 La. St. Normal 0
0 Okla. City U. 7
13 SW La. Institute 27
0 Louisiana Col. 0
26 Cornell (Iowa) 0
7 Centenary Col. 14
0 SE La. Col. 0
98 163

1939 (5-6-0)
Coach: Ray E. Davis
Capt.: Jack Jaggers
32 Ark. A&M 0
11 Wesleyan 7
39 Ala. St. Tchrs. 0
7 West. Ky. Tchrs. 20
6 Brmnghm.-Sou. 7
0 La. St. Normal 26

13 U. of Tampa 0
6 SW La. Institute 12
10 Louisiana Col. 9
0 Tex. Col. of Mines 27
0 Centenary Col. 19
125 127

1940 (6-4-0)
Coach: Joe Aillet
Capt.: Pirkie Vise
1 Louisiana St. 39
0 Oua. (Ar.) Col. 17
19 Tex. Col. of Mines 7
7 West. Ky. Tchrs. 6
0 La. St. Normal 13
20 Ill. Wesleyan 14
6 SW La. Institute 7
15 Louisiana Col. 0
6 Centenary Col. 0
106 109

1941 (5-4-1)
Coach: Joe Aillet
Capt.: Garland Gregory
0 Louisiana St. 25
0 Tex. Col. of Mines 7
0 Auburn U. 34
10 La. St. Normal 0
21 SE La. Col. 14
12 SW La. Institute 7
45 Louisiana Col. 0
0 Hardin-Simmons Univ. 47
39 Centenary Col. 13
7 ... 0
134 112

1942 (6-3-0)
Coach: Johnny Perrit
20 Tex. Col. of Mines 0
45 Waco Army Flying Sch. 0
26 Marshall (W.V.) Col. 0
46 Sam Houston St. 0
13 La. St. Normal 10
7 SW La. Institute 12
56 SE La. Col. 14
13 Hardin-Simmons Univ. 47
33 Memphis St. Col. 7
252 90

1943 — Football discontinued

1944 (3-5-1)
Coach: Joe Aillet
Capt.: Johnny Bibb
0 SW U. of Texas 26
6 Selman Army Air Field 13
72 Marine OCS, N.Orleans 2
0 4th Infantry, Ft. Benning, Ga. 33
0 SW La. Institute 15
21 La. St. Normal 7
14 Ark. A&M 20
0 La. St. Normal 0
7 SW La. Institute 114
120 114

1945 (6-4-0)
Coach: Joe Aillet
Capt.: Bobby Aillet, Herb Scheme
0 SW U. of Texas 26
7 L.K. Charles Army Air Fld. 2
32 Howard (Ala.) Col. 6
14 SW La. Institute 12
21 U. of Miss. 26
20 SW U. of Texas 14
7 Barksdale 7
7 NW State 13
13 SW La. Institute 13
0 Auburn U. 29
133 123

1946 (7-3-0)
Coach: Courtney "Mike" Reed
6 Miss. Sou. 7
13 Howard Payne Col. 7
33 Louisiana Col. 6
38 Ark. St. (Conway) 6
0 U. of Miss. 6
34 NW State 7
14 SE La. Col. 22
2 Okla. City U. 6
34 SW U. of Texas 20
195 87

Several Tech football players under Coach Aillet were drafted by professional football teams. Not all of them made rosters, but a few even became Hall of Famers. Garland Gregory played on the inaugural team of the San Francisco 49ers. George Doherty played for the Brooklyn Tigers, Boston Yanks, Buffalo Bills and New York Yankees. Caleb Martin played

THE BILLY MOSS AWARD

McCoy

Glover

Billy Moss

Perhaps the most coveted award given annually to a Louisiana Tech football player is the Bill Moss Memorial Award presented each year to a player who "best exemplifies the qualities of integrity, character and dependability" shown by the late Billy Moss.

The son of Mr. and Mrs. W. C. Moss of Sulphur, Billy was a standout guard at Tech in the early 1950s and had completed his eligibility when killed in an automobile accident in June, 1956.

"Billy was an outstanding athlete, very determined and aggressive, and he was also an outstanding and very likeable young man," recalls assistant athletic director Jim Mize. "He was quiet and led by effort and example."

Talton

Slack

Past winners of the Billy Moss Award are:

1956 — Charles Glover, center	1964 — Bob Jolet, end
1957 — J. W. Slack, halfback	1965 — Gerald McDowell, fullback
1958 — Bobby Hinton, tackle	1966 — Tommy Linder, fullback
1959 — B. K. Miller, fullback	1967 — Jim Willis, center
1960 — Billy Ware, center	1968 — Walter Causey, def. end
1961 — Billy Jack Talton, guard	1969 — Tommy Spinks
1962 — Paul Labenne, halfback	1970 — Roger McCoy
1962 — Wally Martin, guard	1971 — David Brookings

Jolet

Ware

Hinton

Brookings

Labenne

Martin

Linder

Willis

Causey

Spinks

Miller

McDowell

TECH'S PAST ALL-CONFERENCE MEN

1948 — Jimmy Harrison, halfback
Jack Kelly, tackle
Ed Stassi, guard

1949 — Jimmy Harrison, halfback
Lenny Vogt, tackle
Ed Stassi, guard
Leo Sanford, center

1950 — Gene Knecht, fullback
Melvin Barney, guard
Leo Sanford, center

1951 — John McMichael, def. halfback
Wyman Collie, linebacker

1952 — Ken Bates, off. end
Gordon Brown, def. end

1953 — James Oliver, fullback
James "Buster" Lum, tackle

1954 — Jesse Storts, guard

1955 — Milford Andrews, quarterback
Russell Rainbolt, halfback
Charles Anderson, end
Tommy Hinton, tackle
Pat Hinton, tackle
Bobby Stone, guard
Charles Glover, center

1956 — Tommy Hinton, tackle
Pat Hinton, tackle
Bobby Stone, guard
Charles Glover, center

1957 — Tommy Hinton, tackle
Allen Stough, guard

1958 — Paul Hynes, halfback
Henry Delony, tackle
Charles "Buck" Stewart, center

1959 — Max Rudd, fullback
J. W. Slack, halfback
Charles Garris, end
Bobby Hinton, tackle
Joe Hinton, guard
Jim Campbell, center

1960 — Mickey Slaughter, quarterback
Max Rudd, fullback
Paul Hynes, halfback
Tom Causey, end
Herschel Vinyard, tackle
Joe Hinton, guard

1961 — Mickey Slaughter, quarterback
Jerry Griffin, end
Herschel Vinyard, tackle

1962 — Mickey Slaughter, quarterback
Paul Labenne, halfback
Jerry Griffin, end
Richard Enis, guard

1963 — Billy Laird, quarterback
Wayne Davis, end
Richard Enis, guard
John Robert Williamson, center

1964 — Billy Laird, quarterback
Gerald McDowell, fullback
Corky Corkern, halfback
Wayne Davis, end
Robert Malone, tackle
James Boudreaux, tackle

David Bass, guard
Paul Clark, center

1965 — Billy Laird, quarterback
Robert Brunet, off. halfback
Wayne Davis, off. end
James Boudreaux, off. tackle
Dan Irby, def. tackle
Paul Clark, center

1966 — Eddie Taylor, off. halfback
C. T. "Speedy" Campbell, def. end
Joe Peace, linebacker

1967 — Robert Brunet, off. halfback
Tommy Spinks, off. end
Alden Reeves, def. safety

1968 — Terry Bradshaw, quarterback
Ken Liberto, off. halfback
Tommy Spinks, off. end
Jess Carrigan, off. tackle
Glenn Murphy, off. guard

1969 — Terry Bradshaw, quarterback
Larry Brewer, tight end
Tommy Spinks, split end
Butch Williams, off. tackle
Mark Graham, defensive safety
Johnny Richard, def. tackle

1970 — Ronnie Alexander, linebacker
Ken Lantrip, quarterback
Eric Johnson, split end
Mark Graham, safety
Chris Richardson, nose guard
Tommy Lanius, defensive tackle

for the Chicago Cardinals. Gordon Brown was drafted by the Cardinals but instead played for the Calgary Stampeders in the Canadian Football League. Tom Hinton played for the British Columbia Lions in the CFL. Paul Hynes played for the Dallas Texans and then the New York Titans. John Robert Williamson played for the Oakland Raiders and Boston Patriots. David Lee played for the Cleveland Browns and Patriots. Both Billy Laird and Jim Boudreaux played for the Patriots at the same time Vic Purvis of Southern Miss was there; Purvis, the nephew of former Southern Miss standout Leo Purvis, had been responsible for defeating the Bulldogs when Laird and Boudreaux were in school.

A source of pride for college athletics was the Gulf States Conference All-Sports Trophy. Winners of the annual trophy ranked highest in all sports for the season. This was determined by a point system based on the final position of each sport in the season: five points for first, four points for second and so on until the fifth position.[100] Tech won the trophy in the 1958–61 seasons of sports.

An examination of Coach Aillet's football record at Louisiana Tech reveals the success he accumulated over two decades plus. Yes, he cared about his players and coaching staff and sought to provide an environment for them to succeed academically, physically and develop into fine gentlemen. He also was a monstrously successful football coach. In twenty-six seasons, his 151-86-8 record placed him among the highest ranks of Louisiana college coaches. In the GSC, there was little competition. Two coaches' GSC careers closely followed Aillet's. Aillet coached twenty-five more games than Stan Galloway, who coached at Southeastern, and fifty-two more games than Les DeVall, who coached at McNeese; his .729-win percentage topped the conference. His teams won the LIC three times out of six seasons in the conference, finishing second three other times and finishing third in the year before football was discontinued in 1943 due to World War II. One of his worst years was 1944, finishing with a losing record of 3-5-1. Out of eighteen seasons in the GSC, his teams won nine conference championships, seven of which came in the '50s and shared the title five times. There were four second-place finishes, two third-place finishes and a couple of seasons with losing records, marking only three seasons in a twenty-six-year career to finish with losing records. The overall win percentage at .633 is impressive for such a long career, especially considering several coaches with better percentages did not coach as long. When conference win percentages are examined, however, Aillet demonstrates a higher mark of efficiency. His 20-6 LIC record lands him at .769, while his GSC record of 70-25-3 leaves him at .729. His teams scored 313 more points than opponents scored on them in the LIC, as Tech had 515 points scored versus 202 points scored on; in the GSC, his teams scored 740 points more than opponents scored on them, with Tech scoring 1,874 points to opponents' 1,134 points.

Above: All-Sports Trophy, 1958–59. *From left to right*: Coach Huey Williams, Athletic Trainer Glenn Tilley, Coach Joe Aillet, Coach Jimmy Mize, Coach Cecil Crowley, Coach Barry Hinton (baseball) and Coach George Doherty. *From the Louisiana Tech Sports Communication Department.*

Right: A happy Aillet after finishing Gulf States Conference champions in 1959. *From* The Lagniappe, *1960.*

A few of Aillet's duties and actions as athletic director were scheduling games for all sports and being chairman of the games committee for the Louisiana Intercollegiate Track Meet hosted by Poly in 1940. L. di Benedetto of New Orleans served as referee;[101] a longtime friend of Aillet's, he arranged for Pat Garrett to run in the Sugar Bowl Classic.[102]

As athletic director, Coach Aillet frequently represented the college at conferences. At the 1940 LIC Meeting (where Southwestern was awarded the conference trophy), Vice-President Aillet argued that coaching staffs should not be able to use film from another school's coaching staff in the current season in preparation for games against conference opponents. This practice, like the other potentially unethical behaviors discussed, was banned at the meeting.[103]

Coach Aillet was behind the formation of the Gulf States Conference in 1948, becoming its first president, and was reelected the next year. That year, Mississippi Southern unintentionally generated its own share of controversy. The champions of the Gulf States Conference had two players who had signed professional contracts to play baseball. The central question of eligibility caused amendments to be made to the constitution of the new conference related to this issue. Coach Aillet, as president, had a share of committee work in the affair.[104]

In 1949, the colleges became separated in athletic competitions in an east–west orientation, Tech being in the west with most of its traditional foes.[105] In 1950, Aillet was on the GSC committee to determine the allowance of McNeese College (now McNeese State) into the conference.[106]

A controversy arose between Tech and Centenary in 1963 when Coach Aillet refused to allow the tennis team to play against the Gentlemen because they had a woman on the team. There was no women's tennis team in collegiate competition currently in the GSC. He did not believe it was fair to have them compete against women, feeling that it put the male athletes in an awkward position. He cited a similar event occurring a few years earlier, involving Clifford Ann Creed, one of the top women's golfers in the world, of Lamar Tech (now Lamar University), where she beat a male competitor from Centenary in golf. The Gent player said that he did not feel comfortable in outplaying her, which affected his game.[107]

In one of his last duties as athletic director, Coach Aillet hosted the 21st Annual Track and Field GSC Championship. Harry Turpin was named honorary referee "[b]ecause he has done so much for the Gulf States Conference and for athletics in general,"[108] said Assistant Athletic Director Jimmy Mize. Turpin had been an early supporter and advocate of the formation of the GSC. Aillet would receive the same honor from the GSC at the 23rd Annual GSC Track and Field Championship in 1971, held at Northwestern.[109]

Before the start of the 1940 season, Coach Aillet was honored by an invitation to coach the North Louisiana team in the Louisiana 1940 High School football All-Star Game. Coaching the South Louisiana team was none other than his recent boss, Rags Turpin.[110] Aillet would for a second time coach one of the teams in the Louisiana high school all-star game in 1944.

A project in 1950 to expand the stadium with new bleachers shifted students and the home team to the east side of the field and updated the press box for more room for radio broadcasts of games.[111] The Louisiana Tech Sportswriters Association gave the new press box a rating of "superior," after having made the mistake of giving it an "awful" rating in a previous meeting.[112]

The ever-busy Coach Aillet took on more leadership roles. As secretary of the North Louisiana Rally Association, he was part of the 1950 committee that established classifications for all schools competing at literary and athletic events hosted by the university for high schools.[113] A high school golf tournament was instituted in 1950; it remained the only competition of its kind for high school golfers in the state for several years.[114]

Production of a new, modern, large-scale athletic plant was underway in 1966. The new facilities, the present location of the football stadium, fieldhouse and track were to play a monumental role in the memory of Coach Aillet. "It is something that a few of us have been hoping for, for years and years," said Coach Aillet. "Expansion of our athletic plant is necessary."[115]

At the same time, only two games in 1966 were to be played at home. Coach Aillet explained, "This heavy road schedule comes at a fortunate time since we have no parking at our stadium and construction projects are underway nearby. We can tolerate these inconveniences because we are looking forward in 1967 when we expect to be in our new stadium."[116]

The rules of college football changed frequently during Aillet's tenure. A few key rules greatly affected Tech's playing ability. NCAA rules changes for the 1941 season made for a potentially brighter future. Allowing the ball to be handed forward behind the line of scrimmage would benefit the T formation, another offensive system in use by Aillet. "If we can get some fast backs, the new ruling will also aid us in some of our reverses."[117]

Also, players were now allowed to substitute in and out in the same quarter, and passing the ball on fourth down would no longer require the ball to be put on the 20-yard line in the red zone. Such changes would allow for more innovation, especially in the passing game.

A 1953 NCAA change essentially stipulated a ban of the two-team (two-platoon) system of football. To curtail what was seen as a sport becoming too competitive and trending away from academic focus and integrity by college presidents, players had to play both ways and, if subbed out, could only return in the next quarter of play. One method used by Coach Aillet to keep up with who was eligible was to have color assignments for his players on the bench.[118] This did not greatly affect Tech, as most of its athletes already played both ways, but still meant an overall refinement of the offense and defense. "It's the one-way man that we're concerned about," said Coach Aillet, "and we want to give them every possible opportunity to develop those offensive and defensive skills they haven't used in the last year or two."[119]

The substitution issue would linger for almost a decade. A new rule going into 1960 known as the "wildcard substitution rule" partially rendered the old substitution rule of 1953 obsolete. While "platoon football" remained banned, coaches could send single substitutes after a play was over. If more than one replacement went out, the old substitution rule would then apply. The previous year, 1959, saw the 1953 rule adapted to allow two substitutions by a player for one quarter that he either started in or subbed into before the old rule applied. Now, instead of just two times, a single player could sub in at any time of the game. The only catch was that the player had to play a full play and had to sit out for a full play when returning to the sideline. Another rule change of consequence permitted players subbing from the sidelines to relay messages from the coach; previously, no "coaching from the sidelines" was allowed.[120]

A rule change in 1963 regarding substitutes promised to heap more confusion than the previous alterations and realterations. Teams were now allowed to substitute as many players as possible only on second or third down. Only two could be substituted on fourth down or first down when ball possession switched. Otherwise, more substitutions than that in those situations would result in a 5-yard penalty or would be permitted with a timeout. Most of this was the result of an ongoing feud between proponents for or against coaching from the sideline. Some thought that this new change would help cut down such "interference," while others sought ways to get around the rule as they had with previous rule changes. Another rule change allowed the player taking the snap to become an eligible receiver, allowing the game to further open to more passing options.[121]

A new GSC rule prior to the 1965 season banned noisemakers. One reason for Tech's struggles at the time could be the outlawing of the cannon. The Sigma Nu fraternity had a homemade cannon, which was fired after Bulldog scores both at home and some away games. An observation concluded that every game the cannon was present resulted in a Tech victory; the Southern Miss game of 1964 saw the cannon refused entry. While Tech lost that game, they beat Northeast (now ULM) one week later with the cannon.[122]

Two concerns, aside from the routine filling of roster positions, harried the coaching staff relating to rule changes going into offseason training in 1965. One was a return of unlimited substitution, or platoon football, as had

Stafford Vallery of Plain Dealing constructed the cannon for Engineering Day in 1963; it became adopted by the Sigma Nu fraternity, to be fired when Tech scored. *From Tech Talk, 1964.*

been the norm prior to the 1953 substitution rules, while another was an adaptation to blocking rules.[123] Each of these changes forced college teams to respond. "Because of having to play two-way football in the past, we are in a position that our better offensive players are also our better defensive players,"[124] said Coach Aillet. In each case, where the Bulldogs were forced to play one-way ball and then go back to specialization, Tech was at first negatively affected but learned quickly to adapt.

Coach Aillet was elected Coach of the Year in the GSC four times: 1949, 1955, 1959 and 1964. Ironically, future Hall of Famer Joe Aillet in 1955 was selected for the College Hall of Fame Committee by Ray Eliot, coach of the Fighting Illini of Illinois.[125] Another position he acquired in '55 was deputy commissioner of "midget football" in the Pop Warner Conference. A program designed for youth twelve years old or younger and weighing up to one hundred pounds, its goal was to promote safety in teaching boys the game of football. Positions on these organizations put Coach Aillet in continued contact with some of the premier college coaches of the day, many of whom he was already acquainted with.[126]

Adding to his honors, Coach Aillet was selected by Coach Jess Neely of Rice for membership in the Public Relations and Press Committee of the American Football Coaches' Association in 1956.[127] He became a part of another organization by gaining membership to the board of coaches tasked with rating small colleges for the United Press International in 1958.[128]

The 1939 Northwestern team was celebrated at the Ark-La-Tex Sports Award Banquet in 1961.[129] Aillet received another honor in 1963 by being appointed to the coaches' committee tasked with awarding the Amos Stagg Award to a deserving player to honor the player-coaches' example and influence of life and football.[130] Coach Jimmy Mize became assistant athletic director in 1963 to help Coach Aillet's increasing workload.

Joe Aillet in 1956. *From the Louisiana Tech Sports Communication Department.*

The 1957 preseason events saw the Louisiana Tech head coach traveling with Mike Reed's father to accept the former players' award into the NAIA Hall of Fame. Also inducted was Harry Turpin, recently retired from his head coaching position at Northwestern State.[131]

In 1959, Coach Aillet, in recognition of his then thirty-five-year career coaching football, was selected in the NAIA Hall of Fame. At the time of his induction, his record at Tech stood at 111-59-8; in conference play, including LIC competition, he stood at 67-18-3. Seven times his Bulldogs won titles, won a share four times, finished second six times, third once and fourth once.[132]

Coach Aillet was awarded the Deep South Coach of the Year by the American Football Coaches' Association in January 1965 and was earlier awarded Coach of the Year by the Shreveport VFW.[133]

The State Board of Education in 1965 recommended several new steps aimed at regulating college sports, such as the appointment of a state commissioner of athletics and supported an increase of eighty from sixty scholarships for the GSC along with full NCAA membership of all schools in the conference; Tech was the only member of the NCAA.[134] Stan Galloway, once a successful adversary coaching at Southeastern and currently the GSC president, would become the first state commissioner.

The honor that meant perhaps the most to him came at halftime during the 1963 homecoming game against Southwestern. Numerous former lettermen of all sports at Tech and former T Club members were motivated to give a celebration for his accomplishments, known as "Joe Aillet Day." With Leo Sanford as master of ceremonies, Coach Aillet was honored at the halftime show. Congressman Joe Waggoner, one of the speakers and an alumnus of Tech, emphasized Coach Aillet's character, concentration, courage and commitment to the better things of life. "He is building bridges to the future in these young men's minds," said Waggoner. President F. Jay Taylor said, "We are honoring a man who symbolizes the living spirit of athletics at Louisiana Tech, a man who as earned our respect and admiration."

A deeply moved Aillet left the stage by saying, "I don't hold myself up as a model of modesty, but I wish I felt I deserved all of this." In thanking his family, he said, "There should be a special place in heaven for coaches' wives

Joe Aillet and Louisiana Tech president F. Jay Taylor on parade for Joe Aillet Day. *From the Louisiana Tech Sports Communication Department.*

Above: Taylor at the mic during the Joe Aillet Day halftime ceremony; Joe and Ruby are seated behind with other dignitaries, including on the left Robert Curry and Enoch Nix, members of the State Board of Education, and Mayor Johnny Perritt, a former Aillet player. *From the Louisiana Tech Sports Communication Department.*

Left: Aillet telling quarterback Billy Laird to set his feet before throwing at the 1963 Southwestern game. *From* The Lagniappe.

Opposite: Aillet presented with gifts. *From the Louisiana Tech Sports Communication Department.*

and since I am worse than most coaches, my wife deserves a higher niche. I leave this mic now with a great deal of love in my heart for all of you."

Gifts such as a color TV, suit, golf cart, golf clubs, luggage set, car, trailer and bouquet of roses were presented to the much-appreciated denizen of Louisiana Tech and his loving wife, Ruby. Thanking the crowd, he said, "These material gifts are grand, and I will use them with a great deal of personal pleasure, but I cherish most the sentiment behind them."[135]

As the ceremony concluded, the band formed the coaches' last name on the field and played the alma mater.[136] After the first Joe Aillet Day, Coach Aillet surprised Coach Mize with his own gift. Aillet had received a new Cadillac and essentially gave Mize his '53 Chevrolet, selling it for one dollar. Back then, it was a huge deal to have more than one car. Coach Mize drove it until he retired in 1977.[137]

CHAPTER 9

PLAYER-COACH RELATIONSHIPS

When Coach Aillet returned to familiar North Louisiana territory, he encountered several challenges. The Louisiana Poly Bulldog football program was in turmoil. Among a general shakeup of the athletic staff, former head coach Eddie McLane was stepping down from his role as athletic director and Ray E. Davis, head coach of the 1939 football team, had resigned.[138] McLane and his staff were injured in an automobile accident while returning from watching the 1937 Sugar Bowl, with McLane being seriously injured, and he coached only one more year. He retained his role as athletic director and was replaced as head football coach by Davis, one of his former players at Howard (now Samford) College in Alabama.[139] Davis, however, had little success with the Tech Bulldogs. After another losing season and an overall "lack of harmony" among the coaching staff,[140] Louisiana Poly looked for a new guide to helm the ship.

The Athletic Committee, tasked with this mission, invited Aillet for an interview. When it came time for him to speak, he made it clear upfront that he was a practicing Catholic and was aware of the area Protestant sentiments and that if his faith would pose an issue, he thanked them for their time and would go on his way. President Edwin Richardson of Poly deferred to Dr. John "Tony" Sachs. He informed Aillet that he was from Chicago and a Reformed Jew and had spent several years in Ruston as an English professor. He assured the Cajun that if he as a Jew could live in Ruston, it would be no different for a Catholic. Dr. Sachs had spent his entire life in Chicago before taking a train to interview for a position at Louisiana Tech with President Richardson, also a University of Chicago alumni, and had almost the exact same conversation in relation to his Jewish faith. Coach Aillet nodded, smiled and said, "Gentlemen, let's continue."[141] The culture shock he experienced was like if not more profound than Aillet's.

Dr. H.J. "Tony" Sachs. *From* The Lagniappe.

Dr. Sachs remembered meeting Coach Aillet at his home:

> *I thought I was going to go in and meet the man in the sweatshirt with a whistle around his neck. This gentleman answered the door. He had on a coat and tie…we went into the living room and there was a piano over here and it had opera music on it. Then we went into his den to have coffee and he had the words of Shakespeare there. There wasn't any junk stuff up there or any foolishness. This was who he liked—this is who he was.*[142]

What was to be a thirty-minute visit turned into a three-hour visit. It would start a lifelong friendship between Aillet and Sachs and the others present.

Aillet's musical background began early as a member of the orchestra band and Dramatic Club at Holy Cross. At Holy Cross, St. Edward's and Southwestern, he sang in the Glee Club as a soloist and member of the quartet and engaged in the brass orchestra at the first two schools; each Glee Club toured the New Orleans and Austin areas performing. Aillet was also a member of the Surpliced Sanctuary Choir and the Vested Choir at St. Ed's.[143] Finally, he found time to teach himself piano at Southwestern.[144]

Later, in 1970, when Dr. Sachs was eloquently praising Coach Aillet at his second Joe Aillet Day for his retirement, he quoted a passage from the poem "Abu bin Adhem." The title character is visited by an angel. He asks the angel how favored he is with God, receiving a poor response. At this, he tells the angel to say that if anyone should ask of him, let it be known that he loved his fellow man. The next night, he finds out that his name is among those favored with God. When Coach Aillet stood up, he said, "Well, Tony, thank you for those kind words, but I am no Abu bin Adhem

Top: Holy Cross Glee Club, 1923. Aillet is first from left on middle row. *From the* Holy Cross Gold and Blue.

Bottom: St. Edward's Glee Club, 1925. Aillet is second from left on bottom row. *From the* St. Edward's Tower.

and I don't think my name is at the top of the list."[145] It is safe to say that few, if any, in the room knew the poem or its meaning.

Perhaps lesser known than his propensity for Shakespearean references was his learnedness in the Bible. Having read the Bible six times front to back,[146] Coach Aillet had a profound knowledge of Christianity. His speedreading undoubtedly aided him in his endeavors, as did his photographic memory.

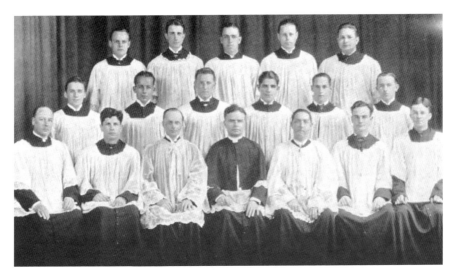

Surpliced Choir, 1925. Aillet is middle top row. *From the* St. Edward's Tower.

Every conversation over the phone was recorded in shorthand, and he could repeat what each player did or did not do in a football play.[147]

Dr. Sachs often referenced Coach Aillet to his students. "I can talk to you about any subject for hours. I can speak to any person in the world for hours. I'm by far the most intelligent guy at Louisiana Tech, although Coach Aillet is a close second!"[148]

Coach Aillet occasionally filled in for professors who had to miss a day, primarily English professors such as Dr. Sachs and Dr. Robert C. Snyder.[149] During the football season of 1941, Coach Aillet was elected to take Dr. Sachs's place on the Student-Faculty Relations Committee, an organization linking students to faculty for issues of campus life. Aillet and Crowley, especially Aillet, were well liked and respected by the student body as soon as they arrived on campus back in 1940. He had been responsible for rousing an interest "that was heretofore lacking."[150] Aillet also became the vice-president of the Louisiana Intercollegiate Conference, another high honor for his early career at Poly, and a collegiate head coach and athletic director.

Outside of football, Coach Aillet enjoyed the company of a small group of men in town: Dr. Ben Everist, a pediatrician; Dr. Kenneth Grubbs, an economics professor; and Dr. LeMoyne Bleich, a doctor and sergeant in the army who survived the Bataan Death March in World War II and husband of Anne Bleich. When Coach Aillet referenced Abu bin Adhem,

Dr. Bleich replied that those people who looked after their fellow POWs were often those who survived. They shared a belief that, regardless of religion, all had a duty to care for one another. The men drank coffee at the Green Clinic Library and shared philosophies. Those meetings were some of the times where they could become passionate yet remain respectful of other's views.[151]

Aillet's athletic résumé up to that point included playing for some of the most respected coaches in college football and demonstrating an ability to successfully coach both high school and college teams. He also earned a reputation for being a molder of boys and men. His leadership in establishing the Louisiana High School Coaches Association added to his reputation and prestige. The extensive knowledge of Shakespeare exemplified the quality of education he received, thanks to Father Rouget and the Congregation of Holy Cross. The man known as a tough, rugged gridiron warrior was also known as "Gentleman Joe" and "the Smooth One."

Many an athlete was confounded by a conversation with the Smooth One, especially in his sacred office of Memorial Gym. His vocabulary gave him much leeway to work with when talking to players.[152] Players never wanted to be called in to Coach Aillet's office. His reputation was enough to keep several athletes from misbehavior, aside from the desire to not displease their endearing mentor. It was not uncommon for a group to leave, and one young man say, "I didn't understand what he was saying." Another might reply, "You stupid, he was chewing our butts out for misbehaving." The first one might protest, "He used those big words, I didn't understand it." "Well," says the second one, "I barely understood, but I know what the bottom line was!" One time, Billy Jack Talton and his roommate and high school teammate from Minden, Wayne Parker, were on their way to Memorial Gym. Parker said, "Look at that on the backseat! In the backseat of Coach Aillet's car was an 'intellectual book' that had become a movie starring Marlon Brando. Who reads books like that?" Talton said, "He does—to relax!"[153]

Richie Golmon was part of another group of eight to nine athletes called in to an infamous meeting at Memorial Gym. There was Coach Aillet, a cigarette held between thumb and index finger, cocked back. "Boys, the reason I called you into the office is, I've checked with your professors, and some of y'all are kind of not doing that well in class. I'll go around and tell you what the problem is." When he came to Buster, he was serious. "Buster, I know what your problem is." "What's that, Coach?" he asked. "You've been participating in cards too much." Buster hopped up, protesting, "But Coach, I

70

haven't been to Moon's! I haven't been to Moon's!"[154] Moon's was a popular place to get beer at Cheniere Inn, between Ruston and Monroe, frequented in those days by college students.

Coach Aillet commanded a lot of respect from the coaches as well, even if they, on occasion, were nervous around him.[155] Billy Belding, the cross-country coach and track assistant, met with Coach Aillet when Coach Mize asked Belding if he was interested in taking the cross-country team to the national championship. After an enthusiastic response, Mize told him to sit and wait while he relayed the request to AD

Taking care of business, 1947. *From* The Laginappe.

Aillet. Belding described Coach Aillet's office as like going to the captain's office in the service, an "inner sanctum": "You didn't sit down until Coach Aillet told you to sit down....You know, I was so nervous, I was making grammatical errors while talking. He would say, 'Oh Billy, you meant to say' such-and-such."

One of Coach Aillet's first priorities when he came to Tech was the need for a new athletic complex. It was one of his signature accomplishments for the university.[156] Among the first orders of business, Aillet brought Cecil Crowley into the program. Crowley led Haynesville to a state championship in 1936 (the team was a runner-up in 1938, his final year). He was fresh from coaching the Male High School of Louisville, Kentucky, and would handle the Bulldog line.[157]

Aillet would quickly prove to be an uncommon football coach. He did not scream and hardly ever blustered. Instead, he conducted himself calmly, quietly. Scholarships for football players were not contingent on a player's ability on the field. Coach Aillet had enough confidence in himself and his coaching staff's ability to evaluate players that if they "made a mistake" in reading a player's ability, players kept the scholarship until they graduated. Beyond this, Aillet and the other coaches would periodically check up on players and help any who needed academic assistance. A source of humor for Coach Aillet in later years were the comments by coaches of opposing teams, who told potential recruits to avoid Tech because they wouldn't be able to make the grades in the classroom.[158]

Louisiana Tech was appealing to the North Louisiana boys who made up the backbone of the team, and the coaches recruited close to home. Coach Aillet was keenly interested in Leo Sanford and invited the youth to the State Fair games and eventually to games in Ruston. Sanford said that one of the best choices he made was going to Tech and playing for the coaches there. One reason he liked going to the games was to sit with the ladies; one lady helped make up his mind when they fell in love and married. Sanford's girlfriend and future wife was set to attend Tech, so that made up his mind over places like LSU or Georgia.[159] She was working in Shreveport, and he wanted to stay close to her.[160]

Tech provided a reliable option for local high school talent. Pat Garrett, son of the legendary L.J. "Hoss" Garrett of Ruston High School, lived a block from Tech Stadium and the track. Having family present and receiving seventy-eight dollars per month for not residing in the dorms, Garrett said, made Tech very appealing.[161]

Billy Jack Talton's reasons for choosing Tech were obvious. Coach George Doherty's success at Minden, winning multiple state championships in the '50s, made him a hot commodity on the coaching market. When he rejoined his alma mater and college mentor at Tech, he all but ensured several quality recruits from Minden. Five teammates went to Northwestern, making for an interesting State Fair matchup. Talton did, in fact, sign with LSU but did not enter, like A.L. Williams. LSU was going after him as a junior in high school. Three of his teammates went. When sixteen-year-old Talton visited the LSU stadium, however, as part of the recruiting trip, he became unnerved. LSU was playing Tulane at a time when Tulane still ran a competitive program in the SEC. Close to sixty-eight thousand fans were in attendance. Louisiana Tech games usually topped off at seven to eight thousand fans in the stadium. Coach Aillet also informed him that the graduation rate of the 1956 national champions was mediocre. Talton signed with Tech—wondering, though, if he would make the team or if he would be smart enough to pass and what it took to achieve what was necessary.[162]

Future Tech head coach Joe Raymond Peace thought that Coach Aillet was the only college football coach. His father, Raymond Peace, played in the '40s for Tech, found his future wife there and had a fantastic career as the head coach of Sicily Island High School. On Saturday morning after a Friday night game, the family would drive to Ruston for a Tech game on Highway 80 (before Interstate 20 was installed). His parents often attended homecoming functions and would come back filled with stories about Coach Aillet's piano playing and singing. When it came time for young Peace to choose between scholarship offers, he never considered any other college. Also, like other player's familial pressures, he figured that his parents would have beaten him if he played for anyone other than Coach Aillet.[163]

One of A.L. Williams's high school coaches, who had played at LSU and tried to recruit him for LSU, told him, "Let me tell you about that coach [Aillet]. He's going to try to see that you graduate and do whatever is best for you. He will do his part." This remark helped make up his mind.

Despite his athletic successes, Williams never really considered attending college until coaches started coming in droves trying to recruit him. It became overwhelming for him, to the point that he asked his high school coach, Clem Henderson, for help. Henderson was an Aillet-coached Bulldog, one of the twenty-two football players who kept their scholarships while serving in World War II.[164] Having no idea about the process, Williams did whatever Coach Henderson told him to do. "If you're asking me where to tell you to go to college, I'm not going to tell you. That's something you got to make up your mind." "Well, I want to play," said Williams. "I don't want to sit on the bench for three years to play." He had previously had a similar experience at the extremely competitive backfield of Fair Park High School. "Well, I don't think it will be a problem," said Henderson.

After Williams had talked with several of the big-name schools of the South, Coach Aillet came in to talk to him. What struck him the most was Coach Aillet's scholarship policy. Unlike the common four-year scholarship discussion he had with other coaches, or lesser scholarships, Coach Aillet explained to him—like he did to so many other athletes—that it was a scholarship until he graduated. "It may take you four, it may take you four and a half, it may take you five. It's a scholarship until you graduate."[165] The coaching staff invited Williams to a basketball game at the opening of Memorial Gym, where he met Scotty Robinson, who in the future would become one of Tech's best basketball coaches.

Mickey Slaughter got a late start to football in high school. After a few good seasons as a converted quarterback from center for Maxie Lambright at Bolton, he did not attract any attention at the collegiate level. Slaughter tried out at several schools' spring training sessions but still got no offers. Louisiana Tech was the last school to invite him, the final opportunity. Because he had gone to high school in Alexandria, Slaughter knew little about North Louisiana colleges, including Tech. He arrived on a Salter Trailways bus, a regional bus line, and had three practice days before being brought to Coach Aillet's office by the trainer on the last day. He expected the usual "Thank you for coming but we don't have anything for you at this time, but if we do, I'll let you know," as the other coaches had said. Instead, a manila folder was sitting on Aillet's desk.

"Come in here. We're going to offer you a full, four-year scholarship to Louisiana Tech in football."

"You've got to be kidding," said Slaughter, looking at him.

He chuckled a bit and said, "No, I'm serious. I think we can make a good quarterback out of you."[166]

Jimmy Orton, who played well in previous years behind Jim McCabe, who graduated, had signed with the New York Yankees. Orton was the heir apparent to McCabe and had "mastered the winged T perfectly."[167] Behind Orton was Taylor McNeel, who played only six minutes the previous year, and freshman Johnny Hudson. In squeezed Slaughter on the 1959 Tech lineup, where he would make his mark.

Bobby Stone was an uncommon member of the team. Not many out-of-state recruits played at Tech, much less from Georgia. Stone played on some of Tifton's finest high school teams. His path to Tech was truly unorthodox. While playing high school football, he became friends with Billy White, who played for the rival school of Fitzgerald. They kept in touch while in college, and both went into military service for the Korean War.

During that time, White, while in the U.S. Air Force, went to clerk typing school at Tech. After watching some of the football games, he talked to Coach Aillet about entering the college. White was discharged before Stone in 1954 and joined the Bulldogs. Stone's line coach from junior college, meanwhile, had caught up to him and convinced him to try out at Texas Tech. After redshirting, Stone and White were returning to their colleges from home after Christmas. White convinced Stone to at least talk to Coach Aillet about transferring after raving on and on about him: "It's like a res camp, you'll like it. Ain't no hollering, no cussing and all that. You'd love it." As the campus was on the way to Lubbock, they stopped and talked to Coach Williamson, who directed them to Coach Aillet's house. He was watching one of the New Year's bowls in the evening. "I can't tell you anything," said Coach Aillet. "You go on back to school, and I'll tell Billy to get in touch with you."

Two weeks after returning to Texas, he called Coach Aillet, who told him to finish out the semester, get closure and come on. Needing to pass twenty-four hours to be eligible at Louisiana Tech, he took classes in the spring and summer and passed twenty-seven hours. Stone, like Talton, enjoyed a smaller environment. He was further impressed by Coach Aillet's emphasis on academics and graduating with a degree.

When J.W. Slack first came to Tech, he did not stay long before going to work on the pipeline for a summer to make a living. Slack quickly found out that the work was unsatisfying and exhausting, and his friends encouraged him to see if Coach Aillet would admit him back in the football program at Tech. After some hesitation, he was surprised to find that the coach would indeed pick him back up, scholarship and all. Not only that, but his wife was helped by Coach Aillet. While she lived in Shreveport, she wanted to move to Ruston to be with Slack but needed a job. Coach Aillet found a job for her as a secretary on South Campus, where the Department of Agriculture and Forestry is located. The couple lived in "Vetville," a collection of apartments on South Campus originally for veterans returning from World War II.[168]

This was not the only time Coach Aillet provided secretarial employment. When Flo Miskelly met Coach Aillet, she did not want to be a secretary in athletics. She told him that she knew nothing about football. "It's okay," he said. "You don't have to because you're not going to be coaching." It turned out to be the best job that she ever had.[169] She would become well known and respected among staff and fans for handling the athletic budget tickets at athletic events during a long, forty-year career at Louisiana Tech. "Here we are, nearly forty years to the day, and she still doesn't know anything about football,"[170] joked Bobby Aillet near her retirement.

The first time Jimmy Mize met Joe Aillet was in Shreveport, when he was caddying in the 1934 Louisiana State Amateur Championship Golf Tournament. One of the players in the semifinals was Joe Aillet, who was coaching at Haynesville. Mize almost attended Centenary and practiced with the team before practicing at Tech under new coach Eddie McLane. Coach Curtis Parker of Centenary was not pleased, prophetically telling him that he would be a "Tech-ite" for life.[171] After playing at Louisiana Tech while Coach Aillet took the assistant coaching job at Louisiana Normal, Mize became an assistant coach with Coach Garrett at Ruston High. Coach Garrett, a fellow Tech alum, was instrumental in Coach Mize's becoming the Arcadia High School head coach. After winning a state championship, Mize entered the U.S. Air Force during World War II and served five years. Coming back in 1946, he was unsure of what he wanted to do. Coach Aillet and Mize met again while Mize was helping Coach Garrett with spring training. Mize reminded him that the two had met at the golf tournament, an event Aillet remembered. It was the start of a lifelong friendship between the two.[172]

Coach E.J. Lewis's first encounter with the Louisiana Tech coaching staff was when Coach Williamson was recruiting in South Louisiana in 1959.

Both being avid hunters, Coach Lewis took Williamson duck hunting; they became good friends. Huey invited E.J. and his wife, Patsy, to Louisiana Tech, which according to E.J. was the best move they ever made. Both worked for Tech and were active supporters. Lewis earned his master's and coached at Jonesboro High School for a few years before returning to Tech as an assistant coach.[173]

Coach Belding, having played high school football in Mississippi and coached for a brief period, was recruited by Coach Mize to leave La Salle High School in Olla, Louisiana, and coach at Tech. He had been approached by multiple colleges about joining the ranks in track. When he talked to Coach Aillet at Tech, he had narrowed his options to Tech and Southwestern. The Lafayette school's track program had a leg up on Tech at that time. "If you want to go for winning, if that's the main purpose in life, then you need to go to USL. If you want to learn more about life, then [you] need to go to Louisiana Tech."[174]

Bill Cox, a Louisiana Tech alum, was a promoter of the college and helped with recruiting; there were several sites in use, the most notorious one being Coach Williamson's hunting camp on the outskirts of Ruston, attracting large crowds. Eventually, following new NCAA guidelines, the recruiting techniques were scaled back.

The Rotary Club Banquet, which capped each season, was always festive. Coach Aillet and Dr. Sachs cooked for it year after year. Cox helped provide entertainment. Aside from card tricks, he brought in Dean Martin and the Golddiggers, the comedians Redd Foxx and Jerry Clower and hypnotists, among others.[175]

Coach Aillet brought in Johnny Lynch, his old friend from Holy Cross, as guest speaker in 1948. After spending some time as a coach at the New Orleans high school, he became a referee.[176] Eventually joining the SEC, he became the only referee to officiate all four major bowls. He would later aid Bobby Aillet in his SEC officiating career.[177] At the banquet, Lynch commented on the superb football exhibited by small schools and complimented Coach Aillet, who was "[o]ne of the soundest coaches in the nation…recognized for his ability in football circles throughout the country."[178]

The 1953 Rotary Club Banquet had as guests Ed McKeever, former head coach of Notre Dame and Cornell and assistant at LSU, and Tech alum Leo Sanford, who narrated a film of a game between the Chicago Cardinals, the team that drafted him in the NFL, and the Green Bay Packers.[179] Dr. Willis M. Tate, president of SMU and former football star at the school, was guest speaker at the Rotary Club Banquet of 1955.[180] At the Rotary Club

Banquet of 1957, among other guests, was Sam Lyle, assistant coach of the University of Oklahoma.[181] Legendary coach Faize Mahfouz of Eunice High School was the guest speaker of the Rotary Club Banquet of 1958, while William Augustus "Dub" Jones; Warren Lahr, his Cleveland Browns teammate; and Leo Sanford were also in attendance.[182]

The guest speaker of the Rotary Club banquet of 1961 was Tom Landry, just having completed his first year as head coach of the Dallas Cowboys.[183] Coach Aillet frequented the Cowboy summer camps as an assistant to keep up to date with development of offensive strategies at the professional level. The Aillet family were welcomed by the president of the Cowboys, Clint Murchison Jr.[184] A.L. Williams asked Coach Aillet what he thought about Tom Landry when Aillet first visited the Cowboys. "If they'll let him alone, he'll be a great winner for them,"[185] was his response.

Aubrey Futrell compared Coach Aillet to Tom Landry; aside from the two coaches' friendship, they carried themselves in a similar manner, and the Cowboys recruiters were in contact with the team.[186] Gil Brandt, renowned Cowboys scout, remembered Aillet well. "He used to come to the Cowboys' training camp, and that was unheard of in the early '60s for a small college coach. Coaches from schools like Michigan would visit, but not coaches from schools like Louisiana Tech. But he was interested in how the pros were doing things, and he and Tom became pretty good friends. You look at high school football in Louisiana now, and it seems like everybody throws the ball a lot."[187]

Receiving awards in 1961 were the Hinton family, honoring their three sons' all-star careers at Tech; Dr. Ragan Green, the team physician; and Leo Sanford, in recognition of his nomination to the NFL Hall of Fame.[188]

Coach Aillet also had a connection with Vince Lombardi that allowed the Bulldogs to visit the Green Bay Packer pro camps for three years, starting in the year the Packers won the first Super Bowl in 1967.[189]

Several former players were at the 1964 Rotary Club banquet. The guest speaker was James Paul Sprayberry, former all-around athlete of Georgia Tech and former president of the SEC official's association.[190] The guest speaker at the 1965 banquet was Blanton Collier, head coach of the Browns, accompanied by assistant coach Dub Jones.[191]

Claude "Gene" Gilstrap, Arlington State athletic director, was guest speaker at the 1966 Rotary Club Banquet. The Rotary Club Banquet contained some extra drama that year. Coach Aillet addressed rumors that he might leave Louisiana Tech for another coaching job. "I have considered leaving," he wearily admitted. "There was some truth in the newspaper article, however I would like to make clear now that I will stay at Tech."[192] This was shortly before his last year coaching football.

A leg up the Tech coaching staff had on recruiting was the ruling of air waves. While Britannia may have ruled the ocean waves, Coach Aillet utilized the flying experience Coach Mize gained in World War II in the Pacific Theater[193] and on the "Himalaya Hump"[194] to fly a Piper Cub—a small, single-engine, two-seater plane—on recruiting duties. The plane was part of the Ruston Aviator Club, comprising flying enthusiasts. Coach Aillet gave the coaching staff assignments for scouting high school games to make connections with coaches and players.[195] Occasionally, Coach Aillet could make multiple trips in a single night to different games.[196] Other times, if Coach Aillet had a LHSCA convention in Baton Rouge or New Orleans, Coach Mize would fly him over.

Coach Aillet knew how to fly as well. His first solo flight was in June 1946.[197] In August that same year, Bobby Aillet made his first solo flight.[198] Coach Aillet flew with player Mike Reed to South Carolina. The original Ruston Municipal Airport was busy when they flew back at the same time as a new training plane that came in for the Veteran's Flight Training (started by Stuckey's Flying Service).[199] The flight program would develop over time into the Louisiana Tech Professional Aviation Program.[200] In November 1946, Coach Aillet became the spokesperson of the newly founded Bulldog Flying Club.[201]

In August 1947, Aillet, having attained his flying license earlier that year, and Mize made a round trip in the Bulldog Flying Club Cruiser in one day to Wisconsin, stopping only once for gas.[202] Another time, he and Coach Mize were flying to a meeting in St. Louis. Halfway there, Coach Aillet landed and switched places with Coach Mize, who took them on to their destination.[203]

Recruiting sometimes involved quirks and unpleasantries. When A.L. Williams was being recruited, it was possible to sign in more than one conference, but not with two schools in the same conference. These were conference letters of intention, not national. "If you weren't going to Tech and anything happened, where would you go?" the Tech coaching staff asked Williams. After he indicated LSU, they told him that it would make no difference then if he signed with them. After Williams signed with LSU, however, it made the papers. Coach Crowley and the coaches at Fair Park became alarmed. One of Williams's sisters had been taught at Haynesville by Coach Crowley. After some diplomacy and politicking with her, Crowley came to Fair Park midmorning. "I thought you told Coach Aillet you were coming!" After Williams explained his conversation with the Tech coaches, which Crowley obviously missed, the Bulldog coach said nothing and left.[204]

In-state recruiting was competitive and mean. LSU, the flagship football program in the state, recruited a center, Don Ellen, already signed with Tech. What made the move particularly egregious, in the eyes of Coach Aillet, was that LSU waited until seeing Eller's performance at the state high school all-star game to pursue recruitment; previously, the Tiger juggernaut had stated that they had no scholarship for him. "If LSU is going to use the prep all-star game held each year in Baton Rouge for last-minute recruiting and luring of athletes away from other colleges that have already signed them, then it might be wise for the state coaches' association to move the game to a site where there is no state college or university or else put it on a rotating basis,"[205] a disgusted Coach Aillet suggested.

He wanted assurances that recruits would not be hounded by LSU officials during the events surrounding the all-star game. Ellen would go on to have a fruitful career at LSU. Already, Gulf States Conference teams were restricted by state law to recruit only in the state of Louisiana; such meddling by LSU greatly harmed programs such as Tech.

Another incident with LSU involved one of Tech's greatest athletes, Tom Hinton, who was hounded by coaches across the South. Al Wimberly of LSU was the main instigator; later, he was one of Hinton's training camp coaches at the BC Lions of the Canadian Football League. During the pro off-season, Hinton and a friend were squirrel hunting in the woods behind his house. Just as his friend found a beehive and tried to get to it, someone called his name. It was Wimberly. After congratulating him on his season, he told him, "I'm still so disappointed that you didn't come to LSU. I could have got you so much publicity and all. It's just a shame that you didn't go to LSU."

"I couldn't be any happier to have gone to Louisiana Tech and the way it's turned out,"[206] responded Hinton. They remained friends over the years despite Wimberly's wishful thinking.

The coaching staff missed some opportunities. Coach Crowley declined to pursue Felix "Doc" Blanchard.[207] Instead, Blanchard would go on to play at North Carolina and then have a Hall of Fame career with Army.

The players recruited by Louisiana Tech came for their love of the game.[208] Carrell Dowies enjoyed the excitement of holding kicks for Joe Michael, his high school teammate from Homer. Being fortunate enough to have the opportunity to play on an Aillet-coached team could sustain a hardened gridiron warrior.[209]

Several generations of families played Tech football, undoubtedly making Coach Aillet feel old. Walter Ford Jr. became the first son of a former Bulldog to play for Gentleman Joe in 1962.[210] After Coach Aillet's time, J.W. Slack's family became the first three-generation family to play for Tech.[211]

Mike Mowad remembered switching from pre-med to education, something that really upset Coach Aillet. By that time, he was retired as a head coach but remained as athletic director. He believed that Mowad should have stuck with his major. Mowad appreciated how much he cared about and took notice of his players' academic pursuits.[212]

Joe Comeaux, living far away from home for the first time, could hardly adjust and planned to leave. The night before he was planning to leave, the RA knocked on his dorm room door to let him know he had a phone call—it was none other than Joe Aillet. After hearing the young man's plans, he made Comeaux promise to come by his office in the morning. "I can't stop you from doing what you think needs to be done," Aillet told him that morning. "Have you told Coach Mize? You owe him the courage to tell him. You owe it to everyone who got you here, the coaches who recruited you and Coach Phillips [his high school coach]."[213]

At the end of the meeting, Comeaux agreed to talk to Coach Mize and finish the semester. Comeaux intended to tell no one of his plans, as he could not face the response. Somehow, Coach Aillet knew that he was struggling. What Coach Aillet cared about more than anything else, however, was the academic achievements of his athletes.

"You come to Louisiana Tech to get an education. You can be good at education and still play football, and play good football, but don't you ever think that you didn't come for an education because we want you to graduate Louisiana Tech with a degree,"[214] said Coach Aillet. Part of the coaching staff's efforts in aiding athletes with their studies involved checking up on them. Leo Sanford remembered Coach Mize knocking on his door, ready to help no matter the problem. Sanford was impressed not only with the coaching staff but also with his teammates, who came for the education and valued it.

For instance, Bobby Aillet and quarterback Ed Jolly, his next-door neighbor in Shreveport, eventually started the engineering firm Aillet, Fenner, Jolly and McClelland with two fellow Tech engineering alumni. "Coach Aillet maintained my interest in keeping up with my studies," said Jolly. "I give him much of the credit for the engineering degree I hold."[215]

Coach Aillet encouraged a fraternal spirit among his players and did not have favorites based on athletic acumen.[216] Carrell Dowies remembered how he was treated like family when he ate supper at the Aillet house.[217] Once a player made the team and stuck with it, he became part of the Tech family. Players were impressed by the caliber of the coaches and how long the program retained them.[218]

Coach Aillet expected the players to wear coats and ties while traveling. "We didn't look like a football team," A.L. Williams said. "People didn't know what to make of us."[219] When asked about his personal attire, Coach Aillet said, "This is my job, and I'm dressing to go to work."[220]

Bill Jones, son of Dub Jones, remembered how Coach Aillet treated them like men. Even when no lectures were given, no theatrical, rah-rah speeches or anything of the sort, they

Looking forward to another year of football. *From* The Lagniappe, *1952.*

knew what he and the coaching staff expected of them. No one told them to be quiet, quit the horseplay and talking, sit up straight and listen. It was an automatic response to his presence. "When he walked in the room, you stopped being a boy, you know, a rambunctious teenager, and you sat up in your chair and you tended to business....Coach Aillet and Coach Mize said, 'Men, take care of your business.' That was a signal that you obviously were not tending to your business at this particular time, and it was time to get serious and tend to what you were supposed to."[221]

J.W. Slack considered himself a good friend of Coach Aillet's and only visited him if he thought the coach could help him with a problem. He did not "bug him" about anything, however. "When he talked, you listened."[222]

"We are not dealing with players," said Aillet, "but whole men. Their ego and development need to be satisfied, and they want someone they can trust and depend upon. When coaching, I used a minimum of rules. All that I asked of the players were that they be prompt, truthful, and courteous. These were the only rules that I set up while coaching. I wanted my players to have a good attitude toward the game of football and toward their teammates, coaching staff, students, and officials. I tried to instill in their minds that football was the greatest game that has ever been invented."[223]

Frequently, Coach Aillet reminded his athletes that they were Louisiana Tech, and whether they knew it or not, their actions reflected on the college. "We were always taught to go to church," said Glenn Murphy. "We were always taught to respect your elders, and you were there for four years to prepare for forty. That was one of his sayings."[224]

Proof of Aillet's gentlemanly conduct and expectations from players is demonstrated in the number of letters he received addressing the conduct of the team, like at Haynesville. Coach Aillet received a letter from the referee of the 1958 Arkansas State game, Paul Hicks, commending him and the team for their good behavior at the game, saying that it was a pleasure to officiate for the school.[225]

It was more important for Coach Aillet to play a gentleman's game than to simply win. The year 1960, Aillet's twentieth season coaching at Tech, was "an unusually harrowing experience." Commending the players, he was glad that they "never got into brawls, play[ed] good, tough football, and although they [were] subjected to a lot of pressures and vicious situations, they control[ed] themselves well and ignore[d] them....While championships are things that we strive for, the most pleasant thing to me is my association with Tech athletes for a long period of years is the fact that they are such wonderful examples of American manhood."[226]

Coach Aillet also commended genteel teams when he encountered them. He particularly appreciated the atmosphere at Cookeville in 1961. "I feel very happy about our new association with Tennessee Tech, and we will be hard-pressed next year to match the hospitality extended to us in Tennessee. Everyone with whom we came in contact in Tennessee exhibited an interest in us and were solicitous in our needs and requirements while there. We even found officials interested in the conduct of the game rather than the type who stand around as spectators. It was a pleasure to compete in an environment that is as wholesome to athletics as that provided at Tennessee Tech."[227]

There were certainly times when the players goofed off. One time, the night before a game at McNeese, Billy Jack Talton and some teammates left the hotel after hours to listen to the Cookies, who were performing a show nearby.[228] When athletes did get in trouble, Coach Aillet disciplined them as a father who cared about his children. Charlie Bourgeois, like a lot of athletes, was too afraid of him to get in trouble, however.[229]

Coach Aillet could sometimes put on a show himself. He was known for his joke-telling, especially during events. Sometimes he could get a good laugh at a player's expense. Once, during practice, Don Tippit was clumsily stumbling and falling, pulling left from his guard position. Coach Aillet told him, "Don, you look like an old washer woman."[230]

Coach Aillet could have fun without appearing to. During one memorable occasion in his later years, the family was gathered at his house for Thanksgiving. His grandchildren played in the yard while the adults conversed. After watching them bounce on yoga balls, he decided he would have a go at it. Walking over, he got one and began bouncing. He bounced all over the yard, not smiling, grinning or looking at anyone. No one said anything, not even the kids, although they enjoyed the show. Finally, upon finishing, he got off and walked back to the adults, sitting down as if nothing had happened.[231]

Coach Aillet was known to be strict, an occasional humorist and entertainer, an intellectual and a fair assessor of talent. He was also an empathetic and merciful coach. One of his players got in trouble with the law and wound up in the parish detention center. The distraught athlete wanted desperately to know if he would keep his scholarship. Knowing the rough background the student came from, Coach Aillet let him know that it would be waiting for him if he got out with a good record. This kind, compassionate act allowed the athlete to go on, play and graduate.[232] Coach Aillet's own childhood gave him a perspective that allowed him to be more supportive of these young men and have patience with them when others might not have been.

People, including his own players, did not always understand Coach Aillet's methods. One time, A.L. Williams asked Coach Aillet about a group of teammates. "Coach, there are some players that really didn't earn their scholarships. They aren't playing enough to. They are seniors and haven't played much. I'm surprised that you keep them."

"That is not their mistake, but my mistake," said Coach Aillet. "You don't offer them a four-year scholarship for an education. They are still doing what they can in school. They are doing well, passing. This is my mistake that I misjudged their ability."[233]

When recruiting Billy Jack Talton, Coach Aillet told him, "If I recruit you and you come to Tech and you can't produce on the football field, you'll still have a scholarship. It won't be your fault, because we're good enough coaches that if you play, we'll get you ready. But if we made a mistake in analyzing your ability to do it, that's our fault and we'll find a way to get you a degree."[234]

In Coach Aillet's coaching style, numerous players excelled. In every play, there was an objective. Aillet never wasted time or energy. Not only did he know what he wanted to do, but the players and the assistant coaches knew as well. He could communicate well with the backfield so that everyone was on the same page.[235]

A seemingly simple but nonetheless meaningful event was the choosing of team captains at the Rotary Club Banquet each year. After the team captains were elected one year, Coach Aillet called J.W. Slack over to let him know

Aillet, also known as "Gentleman Joe" or "The Smooth One." *From the Louisiana Tech Sports Communication Department.*

that he had every vote on the team except one: his own. The unnecessary gesture meant a lot to Slack that Coach Aillet would single him for such praise.[236]

Coach Aillet shared not only his football philosophy but also his life philosophy. During a TV segment, he spoke of a time when he was unable to visit a friend who was not doing well before the friend died. The event made a deep impression on him: "Do not do as I have done. Do not put off visiting a friend in need. Don't wait 'til tomorrow. Do it today. There might not be a tomorrow."[237]

Coach Aillet was not hesitant to throw the football. Even in some clutch situations, such as a fourth and one with time running out, the conventional play would be a run. Coach Aillet did not limit himself, especially when he had quarterbacks of great ability. Much like Coach Garrett, Coach Aillet did not often rely on trickery to accomplish his goals—everything was carefully calculated and based off a careful study of the game and of the opponent, along with consulting assistant coaches.[238] "He moved—I mean, he would change. He would go to one formation to the other to fit his people," said A.L. Williams.[239]

Before the 1940 season, Aillet simply left the subject of the offensive system at "the Notre Dame Box, with variations": "We would rather let our opponents find out about that for themselves, as far as possible."[240] The year 1940 would be the first time Poly and Aillet utilized the "T" formation as well, a formation that had returned to popularity in recent years.

While Tech occasionally ran out of the "T," it really depended on the athletes available as to which systems Coach Aillet preferred. One appeal to the T formation lay with a quick attack that allowed for smaller lines to spread more widely and create more favorable blocking angles,[241] which particularly occurred in the Southwestern game of 1949.

A full transition to the T was in swing in 1951, along with elements of the wingback that worked in '50.[242] One reason for this was a lack of centers whom Coach Aillet believed would be effective in the Box. When asked about the offense in 1953, Coach Aillet said that the T would continue being used if player personnel matched up to it.[243]

Tech in the winged T against Southwestern in 1961. *From* The Lagniappe.

One of the more important changes in 1959 was the offensive realignment to the winged T.[244] Having found success with it the previous year, Coach Aillet made it the centerpiece for the offense. Unlike the switch to the T formation, the Bulldogs did not have much trouble adopting the new system. Providing balance between running and passing, the winged T utilized a split end as an extra receiver and focused on short passes and speedy, often deceptive running; it was not a spread offense with a wide-open pass game or a power running game.

A successful execution of Coach Aillet's three-team regimen was instituted that summer, in 1962. The blue team constituted starters, while the red and green teams comprised the second string and reserves. Another wrinkle to the Bulldog team involved implementing a pro-style offense, one that now centered on passing as the primary mover of the offense.[245]

In preparation for the 1963 season, Coach Aillet did not seem to consider the recent substitution rule change initially, preferring to stick to the three-team mode of play, with blue playing both ways, red the defense and green the offense.[246] At the least, the new rule change was confusing to all. "Two-way football is aged," said Coach Aillet, closer to the season opener at McNeese. "Nowadays, everyone is wanting someone who can do a certain type of work and do it well."[247]

Finding success with the new substitution system used against East Texas State in 1964, the Bulldogs began using a "Red Dawg" group comprising second team players and defensive specialists versus the three-team. The blue and green teams still existed, while the Red Dawgs were used in a defensive role, sometimes including green team players in their ranks.[248]

Another key to Coach Aillet's success was his ability to shift personnel around. For example, Wallace Martin came to Tech playing the fullback-linebacker positions. After teammates were injured, he was moved to a center. When the regular center came back in Martin's senior year, he became a left guard. "I think he maximized the talent that he had at school—I'd say he got the most out of the kids that played for him, and we all had a great appreciation for him."[249]

Coach Aillet often used literature and philosophy to coach. "A sweep is a sweep, is a sweep, is a sweep," he said, alluding to the Gertrude Stein poem "A Rose Is a Rose."[250] Another time, the KRUS radio station in Ruston had a question in a Relay Quiz program about what the score was when Casey struck out, referencing the poem "Casey at the Bat" by Ernest Thayer. Coach Aillet answered correctly, 4–2.[251]

Coach Aillet encouraged his football players to run track, but it was not a requirement.[252] An interesting requirement of the coaching staff, at least in 1963, was that all players be able to run a mile in under six minutes.[253]

Keeping up to date was a must for Coach Aillet. He was known to study sports in the same manner a scholar would attend to his studies.[254] When he wasn't reading, he was attending camps of college and professional teams. These events involved coaches and players from across the country; through familiar associates and new acquaintances, Coach Aillet's football knowledge grew. His reputation as an innovator was part of his overall character as a gentleman. Never content to sit back and continue time-honored traditions, he always looked to the pros and big schools to see what new developments were on the market.

Before the 1941 season began, Coach Aillet attended a coaches' clinic in Baton Rouge.[255] The next year, he attended a summer coaching clinic at the Naval Reserve preflight school in North Carolina.[256] This is likely where Coach Crowley made contacts when he entered the U.S. Navy in 1943.

Sometimes, Coach Aillet hosted camps. Ahead of the 1949 season, a Gulf States Conference coaching clinic was hosted at Louisiana Tech. Although Coach Aillet did not have a lead position in it, he remained busy organizing the early September event that included Johnny Lynch discussing college football rules.[257] In the middle of summer preparations for the upcoming season, Coach Aillet lectured at a Louisiana coaches' meeting on "Player-Coach Relationships" in 1959[258] and hosted a clinic at Tech for high school coaches in the region, bringing in assistant coaches Mike Lude of the University of Delaware and Hal Herring of Auburn. Lude handled discussion of the winged T that Delaware had popularized in recent years to great success, and Herring handled defensive discussions.[259] A few years later, Coach Aillet was the main speaker at the Arkansas High School Coaches' Clinic of 1961, speaking on the winged T.[260]

If he could, Coach Aillet often brought in professional football players to help in preparation for a new season. For example, when Coach Aillet shifted from the split T to the winged T, he brought in Chicago Cardinals quarterback Lamar McCann to help install it.[261] In 1962, the year Tech started playing from a pro-style offense, Bobby Layne, the Pittsburgh Steelers quarterback, came to Tech in the summer.[262]

Glenn Murphy became sold early on with Coach Aillet's strategy. At a team meeting before the start of the 1964 season, Murphy remembered Coach Aillet telling the team, "Gentlemen, we will play McNeese, our first conference game. This will be the first play we run on our first offensive play. We will score a touchdown and we will defeat McNeese and we'll win the

Aldon Reeves with little room to run against McNeese, 1964. *From* The Lagniappe.

Aillet addressing the team during a game. *From* The Lagniappe, *1956.*

conference," before drawing the play on the chalkboard. Every part of his address to the team happened exactly as was stated.[263]

Coach Aillet remained consistent. It didn't matter if the record was 9-1 or 1-9. Tech players who were a part of both teams could hardly tell a difference in his demeanor. He did not terrorize the team when losing.[264] Tommy Linder was thankful to have played for a coaching staff that respected their athletes, unlike other teams he had seen whose coaches screamed at players and were disrespectful to others.[265] That was not Coach Aillet's style; he called people by their first name.[266] Tom Causey also appreciated Coach Aillet's demeanor. He did not respond to yelling very much and came to see the value of Coach Aillet's approach when he began coaching.[267]

While other players and coaches might lose control if the game was not going their way, Coach Aillet rarely, if ever, lost his cool. "Let's calm down and stick to the game plan," he would often say in team huddles. No matter what the occasion, whether it be on the football field or a banquet or presentation, Coach Aillet was always prepared. If a player lost his cool and got kicked out of the game for fighting, some assistant coaches could lose their cool as well; Aillet would go over, calm them down and explain what the game plan going forward would be. "In their respective areas, they were as good as they had in my estimation and I was around a whole bunch of coaches," said Tom Hinton.[268]

No vulgarity was used by Coach Aillet or the coaching staff.[269] "Losing was not pleasant," said Bill Jones. "Playing for him was pleasant. In other words, even in a losing season, there wasn't acrimony. I mean, there was correction, what did you do wrong, I mean, you go over the films. But it was constructive, and maybe that's the word I'm looking for. All the coaching that I saw him do was constructive. That's not universally true."[270]

Sideline discussion during a game in 1962. *From* The Lagniappe.

When Belding was a graduate assistant, Coach Aillet frequently visited with him over the goings-on of the team. Any discussion on how he could improve was always corrective.[271] "He was uplifting. He never ran anybody down," said Wallace Martin.[272]

Jones was impressed by the harmony of the Bulldog coaching staff. There was no friction between them, as he experienced with other coaching staffs. "It is a tribute that they didn't take a head coaching job somewhere else."[273] Another testament to the kind of coaches Joe Aillet surrounded himself with was that Coach Mize allowed Aubrey Futrell to finish out the track season even though he was leaving the college to join the police force of his hometown. Futrell redshirted his freshman year and played his sophomore year in 1967 after Coach Aillet had retired.[274]

Paul Bonin, one of the football captains of 1940, returned the following season to assist Coach Mike Wells with the freshman team. Wells, a former assistant with McLane and then Davis, took Coach Hogg's place, while Hogg took Wells's position as head of the Physical Education Department.[275]

Huey Williamson served Tech well. Williamson, a Tech football alumnus shortly before Aillet arrived, joined the staff in 1951 and had coaching experience at Ruston, Rayville and Ponchatoula High School before becoming a P.E. teacher at Tech.

Joining the regular staff in 1957, Coach George Doherty had played for the Buffalo Bills; as team captain, he once faced off at a coin toss against another Tech player, team captain Garland Gregory of the new San

Francisco 49ers.[276] The Bills won that game. In more recent years, Doherty coached at Stamps High School in Arkansas and took Minden to two state championships.

While only on the coaching staff for the 1966 season, legendary high school coach Lee Hedges assisted Coach Aillet in the backfield before joining Captain Shreve High School in Shreveport. Several players from Woodlawn High School, also in Shreveport, had followed their coach Hedges to Tech in '66, with Terry Bradshaw leading the way.[277]

Large schools were interested in Coach Aillet. Both Ole Miss and Auburn pursued him in the late '40s after multiple seasons where Aillet-coached teams played them well. Auburn presented an interesting option, as he had a connection via Jack Meagher. Aillet lost 34–0 to Meagher's Plainsmen in 1941 and tied Auburn 13–13 in 1948. Ole Miss, however, was the closest he ever came to leaving Tech. He asked the coaching staff if they would join him in Mississippi, to which they replied yes, though not immediately. There were several possible reasons he chose to stay. Cynthia was still in high school, and he did not want to move Ruby around again. Both locations had just as few if not fewer Catholics. He and the coaching staff had also taken a liking to Ruston.[278] When he turned down both offers, he was asked who he thought would make a good coach. In the case of Ole Miss, he said Johnny Vaught, while for Auburn he said Ralph "Shug" Jordan. Aillet's word was not final, but he knew talent when he saw it. Both men would go on to leave their marks for the two universities, as Aillet would for Tech. Two other schools interested in him were Oklahoma and Notre Dame.[279]

While Coach Garrett of Ruston High and Coach Aillet held each other in high regard, their coaching styles were completely different. Coach Aillet experimented with different formations and tailored his offenses to fit appropriately within his early explorations into a "wide-open offense." Coach Garrett stuck with the Notre Dame Box for most of his coaching career, as it fit his smash-mouth power football approach. Their coaching methods also were drastically different and fit with their personalities. Coach Aillet's practice sessions were methodical and almost mechanical. Coach Garrett's were impassioned, extremely physical events. Coach Aillet, of course, was well known for being cool under pressure and sought to instill high discipline and poise. Coach Garrett was fiery and capitalized on passion, desire and the energy of players. Each were well established in their modes of operation yet remained good friends. Several of Ruston's finest players moved on to Louisiana Tech.[280]

Coaching staff, 1966. *From left to right*: Joe Aillet, George Doherty, Jimmy Mize, Huey Williams, E.J. Lewis and Lee Hedges. *From* The Lagniappe.

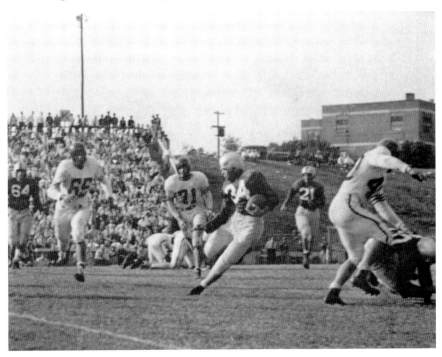

Auburn game, 1948. *From* The Lagniappe.

Coach Garrett received the Distinguished Achievement Award of the Pop Warner Midget Football Conference from Coach Aillet in 1960. Garrett and Aillet were two of the most well-established coaches in the areas—Garrett since 1937 at Ruston High School in football and track and Aillet at Louisiana Tech in football and golf. "I feel that in honoring Coach Garrett," said Aillet, "we are rendering recognition to a man who has perhaps done better for the youth of our city than any other man. It's a pleasure to honor a person who has had such a good influence on young people." Coach Garrett's instruction went "beyond the mere teaching of athletic techniques, serving as a guide to a way of life for hundreds of youths of the Ruston area."[281]

While thoroughly engaged in the affairs of campus life, Aillet was also civically engaged, joining the Lions Club, Rotary Club, Kiwanis Club and Chamber of Commerce. He also encouraged his coaches to join these clubs to contribute to society as much as possible.[282]

Don Tippit remembered seeing Coach Aillet and Coach Doherty at Mass on Sunday mornings. They sat at the second pew on the left, while he sat in the back. There were other teammates like Herschel Vinyard and Jack Lestage who attended Mass together, as well as a growing number of other students, especially from South Louisiana.[283]

Coach Lewis, who arrived after Tippit graduated, had fond memories of church at St. Thomas Aquinas back then. Father Vincent would greet him in the vestibule early before Mass every morning "to tell me what I did wrong with my coaching!"[284]

Whenever the administration changed at Tech, it greatly affected athletics, sometimes for the better and sometimes for the worse. The first such change in Coach Aillet's tenure as athletic director occurred in 1941. Dr. Claybrook Cottingham's tenure at Poly, though short, would see a continuance of growth in several aspects of the campus, not least of which was athletics.[285] Outgoing president Richardson and Coach Aillet were initiated into Omega Kappa, a social fraternity at Poly, that became the Gamma Epsilon Chapter of Sigma Kappa; Aillet would serve as faculty sponsor.[286]

Ralph L. Ropp arrived at Tech in 1949. Ropp and Aillet were friends going back to their time at Northwestern State, Ropp as a professor of forensics.[287] After successful seasons in several sports in 1949, Coach Aillet and President Ropp hoped that school spirit would remain high. Aillet, ever the gentleman, however, believed that organized cheering, led by cheerleaders, encouraged good behavior and discouraged that which was "not becoming of good sportsmanship" such as booing from fans.[288]

President Ropp at a game. *From* The Lagniappe, *1951.*

President Ropp retired in 1962 and would be replaced by one of Tech's most influential and well-known figures, F. Jay Taylor. Taylor, a former Louisiana College official like Cottingham, was young, bold and had huge ambitions for the college. Widely known for his flamboyant personality, he was all-in for Tech. "I have so many plans for Tech that they even frighten me,"[289] he said when addressing the fall convocation crowd in his first year.

President Taylor's vision went beyond that of Aillet's. Coach Aillet had been very pleased about the prospects of Louisiana Tech football going into 1963: "As a result of our successful recruiting, Tech football in the very near future will be back up to the standards of the 1959 club....The Tech football future looks very bright."[290] Taylor predicted a "new golden era of sports." Taylor described plans for updating and expanding, with new tennis, baseball and football facilities among other infrastructure changes. "I hope you like what you hear, because this is the promise of the future."[291]

He was the opposite of Coach Aillet. The elder Cajun was soft-spoken, technical and methodical. No longer would he have a cordial relationship

Opposite, top: Ropp predicting victory in the State Fair Game Parade of 1959 with the State Fair Queen. *From* The Lagniappe.

Opposite, bottom: Ropp addressing crowd before the State Fair Game of 1959, demon dummy on stage. Aillet is sitting behind the podium. *From* The Lagniappe.

Above: President F. Jay Taylor and family in the 1966 SFG parade. *From* The Lagniappe.

Left: Taylor at a game in 1963. *From* The Lagniappe.

with the office of the president. The almost inevitable personality clash would soon spill over into an unofficial cold war between the two. Taylor was part of the growing push for Tech to expand beyond the Gulf States Conference and compete against higher-level competition with the expectation of one day playing "big time football." Such actions would be anathema to all that Coach Aillet had worked for in twenty-two years at Tech; he built up the program and made it prestigious and respected at a national level but did not believe it to be in the school's best interest to push forward so aggressively.

A key example was the 1966 Alabama game. Referred to as a silver-haired David baiting Goliaths, Coach Aillet received national attention for going up against top-ranked Alabama in the upcoming season. "I

Taylor giving the victory signal for the 1962 SFG. *From* The Lagniappe.

have no predictions, but I have a lot of hopes," said Coach Aillet. "We intend to play the finest ball game we possibly can." The playing of such powerhouses was not to be interpreted as a move to big-time football, at least not in the eyes of Coach Aillet. "We're not at that level…however, we're not neglecting any opportunity to play a big-name ball club. We have a fine relationship with a lot of schools. They know we are trying to run a legitimate athletic program and they know we will try very hard to give them a good game."[292]

Several players went on to have successful careers outside of football after graduation. Jimmy Campbell became a dentist and Pat Hinton a general manager at Springhill General Hospital. Joe Hinton earned a doctorate in education and came back to Tech to teach, and Herschel Vinyard became an electrical engineer.[293] They often came back to work at their alma mater. Ora "Ding" Merriott was the first to do so, becoming a physical education teacher in 1947 before returning in 1964 as Student Center director. Garland Gregory came back to teach in the P.E. department in 1966 and started the Recreation Program at Tech in 1970.[294] Gregory would task students with creating a park on wooded land past Joe Aillet Stadium and the future site of Thomas Assembly Center. This project became Hideaway Park and later had its creator's name attached to it after Gregory's death.[295] Billy Jack Talton started a championship powerlifting program in 1974. A.L. Williams coached the 'Dawgs in the '80s, and Joe Raymond Peace followed right after into the '90s. Carrell Dowies served as the associate alumni secretary in the '70s, and Charlie Bourgeois served as the Alumni Association director in the 2000s. Paul Labenne, like Bobby Aillet, officiated for several decades, Aillet in the SEC and Labenne in the Mountain West and Western Athletic Conference.[296]

Coach Aillet never stopped helping his men. Before Joe Raymond made any major professional move, he contacted Coach Aillet. His close connection to Coach Aillet, from his father playing for the coach to Mrs. Aillet babysitting him when he was two to three years old to his playing career at Tech and later coaching career, made him highly value the coach's opinion. His father also encouraged him to talk to Aillet. He even had Joe Aillet work as his agent, handling the negotiations for his contract with the Houston Oilers. Consulting Aillet made him feel better about the decision.[297]

Aillet-coached players became football coaches across the state, affecting lives of innumerable youth. Coach Aillet pushed academics and served as an example of integrity; several of his athletes would go on to become coaches and be involved with kids in health and P.E.[298] Peace's father coached much like Coach Aillet. The temperament was the same—preparation was thorough and orderly.[299]

Mickey Slaughter, ever grateful to Coach Aillet, had planned to join the U.S. Air Force in his father's footsteps. His family, like many others, did not have the resources to send him to college. He also was indebted to Coach Aillet for helping him control his temper and improve his decision-making. All Slaughter had to do was look at his example. Such leadership served as a model when he later went into coaching.[300]

For Tom Causey as well, Coach Aillet's coolness and self-control appealed to him and influenced his coaching.[301] Billy Jack Talton used offenses in his high school football coaching that the Bulldogs ran when he played at Tech.[302]

Pat Collins asked to be a graduate assistant. This position started what would become a Hall of Fame coaching career. "I can't think of a better person in the world to be associated with than Joe Aillet." Collins came to appreciate Coach Aillet's staff meetings. The organized way with which Aillet ran the program, as well as how input from everyone was considered, greatly impressed Collins and influenced his coaching. One piece of advice that Coach Aillet gave to Collins was, "Feather your own nest. Don't worry about what's going on down the road. Worry about what's going on down here."[303]

Wallace Martin remembered how much Coach Aillet used the big chalkboard when he was a graduate assistant. He also remembered Aillet's respect for the professors of the campus. "He did not set himself apart as 'I'm the football coach, you guys are teachers. You are nothing special.'"[304]

"I could credit him with the philosophy I had today, a lot of my coaching philosophy," said Mike Mowad. Ironically, Mike Mowad, a Catholic, almost got his first head coaching job at the alma mater of Coach Aillet—Holy Cross—although he would wind up coming back to Tech as a graduate assistant with Maxie Lambright instead. He was roommates with Mike Lynch, son of John Lynch, thus part of the Holy Cross connection.[305]

"Anyone who ever played for him was influenced by him," said A.L. Williams. "Sometimes you don't even realize it. The day I resigned I wished so much that I could talk to him. I knew he could tell me how to handle the situation. It was the same way when I had to handle a disciplinary problem. The only way I would handle it would be to ask myself, 'If this was my son, how would I handle it?' and 'How would Coach Aillet handle it?' He was so fair and such a genuine person. I tried to be like him and used him as my guide. He taught me you have to realize you're dealing with human lives and not machinery."[306]

Futrell's guiding principles were set by Coach Lewis and Coach Robertson at Jonesboro as well as Coach Mize. Their examples shaped how he acted in law enforcement. Coach Aillet's style of coaching appealed to him. Coach Aillet knew that some players could be yelled at to get the most out of them, while others, such as Futrell, responded better to encouragement. "If Coach Aillet asked me to run through a brick wall, stand by brick wall, here I come! But I've had coaches that would yell at you and tell you to run through that brick wall and I may hit that wall but I'm not going to—you're not going to get 100% effort out of me."[307]

Tech players were not the only ones to benefit from Coach Aillet, who served as master of ceremonies for "Dub" Jones Day in the offseason of 1952. Also in attendance was Hoss Garrett, his high school coach, and Claude "Little Monk" Simons, his Tulane coach.[308] Jones was a standout back at Ruston High School, one of the best players to ever don the red and white. Jones and Aillet knew each other from 1940. In Aillet's first year in Ruston, Jones's family shared a house with the Aillets. Coach Aillet became very familiar with the high school senior's playing ability. Dub Jones had two major connections to Louisiana Tech: Coach Aillet and Bulldog trainer Eddie Wojecki, who helped keep him healthy in high school. Although Jones played at both Tulane and LSU instead of Tech, the two remained friends. As Jones was about to graduate from Tulane, which he attended while in the V-12 program, Coach Aillet did something he would do for many other athletes. Using his connections in the pro football ranks, he gave a player profile of Jones to his old mentor Jack Meagher, then at the Miami Seahawks. While Aillet's correspondence alone did not influence the Seahawks to draft Jones, it undoubtedly helped. Although the Miami franchise was not viable and would soon fold, it provided a springboard for Jones to eventually land with the Cleveland Browns, where he would enjoy a Hall of Fame career as a player and coach. Jones visited Coach Aillet whenever he was in town to discuss football and life.[309]

Jim Henderson, the son of Clem Henderson, was affected by Tech football even though he never played. "The lessons that Dad passed on to me that he learned from greats like Joe Aillet and Jimmy Mize demonstrate the generation-spanning influence of a university devoted to developing students into citizens of a great impact."[310] Henderson would become president of the University of Louisiana Systems in 2017.

Aillet had other duties aside from being football coach and athletic director. Due to the Second World War, the U.S. military began mobilizing in anticipation of conflict; the Bulldog roster felt the burden of several absences in 1941, either from grades or military service. Several colleges, including Poly, were forced to delay opening of the fall semester due to the military games taking place along the highways.[311]

Considering these challenges, 1941 was an impressive year. The Louisiana Poly football team was the only one in the South to have players earning a minimum of twenty-four hours with a C average. In the spring semester of 1942, the athletes had higher grade point averages than social fraternities.[312] Also, the Poly team had more players lost to the draft than several in the region.[313] Several more football players would be lost to military service after the bombing of Pearl Harbor. The ability of colleges to schedule sporting events was hampered.

The conference then took a historic step, allowing unrestricted freshmen to play in varsity sporting events since, due to the war, players were in short supply. This would alter the landscape of sports such as football; previously, freshmen were segregated from the rest of the team and often did not play in regular season matches other than other freshman college teams or high school teams. Now they were included with the regulars.[314] In 1942, there was no "transfer portal" like modern college football, nor were junior college transfers very common. There was a more concerted effort in developing young athletes and less pressure to switch schools, especially under Coach Aillet. In fact, although some of Poly's finest players were transfers, Coach Aillet required a release before allowing them on his team, unlike other competitors, who more aggressively pursued transfers. There would also be no more freshmen-specific coaches either, as Coach Wells was promoted to the regular team, focusing primarily on guards.[315]

Among the growing list of absentees due to the war draft, volunteers or defense workers was trainer Doc Wojecki, who joined the navy in a similar capacity. Taking his place was Billy Cobb, a physical education major and basketball player training under him.[316] Coach Aillet remained confident, however, saying that they were a quiet and serious bunch of young men who were easy to work with and glad to be training.[317]

The game ball of the Poly homecoming game against Southeastern in 1942 was presented to Mrs. Evelyn Meeks, whose husband, Pat Meeks, was killed in action in England.[318] Meeks was a former football and baseball star for Poly. Preserving an undefeated home record by beating Southeastern, 56–14, the Bulldogs had been frustrated by losing to their biggest rivals, Northwestern and Southwestern, the previous games. Coach Aillet was proved right when he said before the game, "Bad luck can't last forever."[319]

There would be extended time to celebrate and ponder the accomplishments of the 1942 season, as all LIC sports were to be suspended until the war was over.[320] The coaches believed that the freshmen players were rushed into the season, unlike previous years, when the first year was spent on development. Therefore, practice continued for the freshmen even in the extended offseason. "If we don't have good football teams in the future," said Coach Aillet, "it won't be because of too little work."[321]

Coach Aillet was a man in perpetual motion. Although he understood why college athletics were canceled, he hoped that high school competitions would continue. Most high school athletes were underage, he pointed out, and sports could keep them physically fit until they came of age. There was also the benefit to classroom harmony in a student body allowed to "let off steam" by playing and spectating. "Interscholastic athletics form the most wholesome and convenient way for school pupils to relax."[322]

Amid friends and family joining the armed forces, Joe Aillet stayed home, although not by choice. When he tried to enlist in the navy, like Coach Crowley,[323] he was not accepted as he did not have the required paperwork such as a birth record. Aillet asked his brother Clarence to help him; they tried to acquire what was required from the New York Foundling Hospital, but they were not successful.[324]

Not letting this stop him, Aillet found other ways of contributing to the war effort. He entered the State Home Guard in 1943 and became a second lieutenant of his company before being promoted first lieutenant.[325] Duties included being on standby to answer the governor if needed to put down riots and protect against invasion or natural disasters. Most of the time spent by the Home Guard was in meetings and drills. Soldiers were furnished with weapons, ammunition and uniforms. Only soldiers on duty received pay. Home Guard units belonged solely to governors; thus, they could not be federalized or moved outside of their respective state.[326] Of course, in the Mayberry-like atmosphere of Ruston, it often did not get more eventful than recovering rifles borrowed for hunting when the unit was dissolved in 1947.[327] The importance of the Home Guard would fill some of the void left by the absence of sports.

Another contribution to the war effort was his involvement in the United Services Organization. The USO provided entertainment to troops stationed in the area. One popular attraction Coach Aillet oversaw was showing films of popular football players and games, as he had done previously at Howard Auditorium on campus and at St. Thomas Aquinas and Trinity Methodist Church. Sometimes he would even provide commentary and give walkthroughs of plays.[328]

Football practice persisted for those who remained, even without games to play. Coach Aillet kept up with his athletes—several of them, from all sports remained scattered across America and the world. They traded letters back and forth, one giving constant updates on sports and other campus activity, while the others spoke what little they could about military life. As before, Coach Aillet's scholarship system was still in place. All twenty-two current Poly football players would retain their scholarships for the duration of the war.[329] Both gridiron warrior and coach longed for the day when peace could be had and life could return to normal. The exciting conflict, tempered with the brutal reality of bloodshed, would one day end and be replaced by the less brutal game of football.

Coach Aillet probably did not envision himself coaching basketball at the college level. With Coach Crowley gone, however, and the chance to bring some sports back, Aillet was to coach the 1944 Bulldog basketball team until multiple players were found to be academically ineligible.[330] It was thought that there would be no more sports until the conclusion of the war; however, football was played in 1944. Aillet coached basketball in the same year, finishing with a 5-12 record.

Most of the members of the 1944–45 teams were V-12 trainees; most of the others were freshmen who would be ineligible until completion of their first trimester at Poly.[331] The V-12 program came into existence due to the shortage of officers at the start of the war; trainees took classes along with the training courses.[332]

As a token of gratitude, Coach Aillet awarded letters to several of the V-12 players. Although they were now dispersed across the world, he would not forget their services through the tough year of 1944.[333] The team had faced numerous impediments to get to this point, and the coaches had a hard time, especially considering Coach Aillet's position in the Home Guard. His leadership and care likewise would not be forgotten.

In the runup to homecoming rituals and the second game with Southwestern in 1945, Mike Reed chose Freida Reed (no relation) to be the homecoming queen; Mike chose her to honor Pearce Didier, her fiancé, and his former teammate before the war.[334] Didier was recovering from his POW experience in Germany. Participating in the Battle of the Bulge, he received the Purple Heart for his wounds in battle.[335]

Before the 1950 season could begin, the Korean War threatened peace. Though not on the same scale as World War II, the Korean War had a similar effect, upending American life again and affecting the ability of football teams to function.

For many players, their best years were spent at Louisiana Tech. Billy Jack Talton met his wife at Tech. He saw her at the cafeteria one day, and he told himself he'd have to ask her on a date. When he saw her again at the student center dance, he was encouraged that she was pretty enough to have a date. Not wanting a confrontation, he waited until her date walked away. "I introduced myself to her and we danced, and the rest is a fifty- or sixty-year history, whatever number of years," said Talton.[336]

Jerry Griffin's girlfriend lived in Aswell, one of the girl's dorms. To let her know that he was coming, he would stomp on a metal drain that led to her room. It didn't lead to any good, however, as soon everybody stomped on it.[337]

"I had always heard that college was the most fun you'll ever have in life," said Aldon Reeves. "It was for me. For five years, I enjoyed every minute of it…I had a '65 Mustang and boy I thought I was king of the hill!"[338]

Richie Golmon enjoyed being able to hunt and fish and also met his future wife at Tech.[339]

Wallace Martin remembered the absence of Interstate 20. Back then, to go to Monroe or Shreveport meant taking Highway 80, which had more traffic and a slower speed limit.[340]

"If I had it to do all over again, I'd want to come right back here to Louisiana Tech, because this is the place where I had so much fun," said Terry Bradshaw when pumping up the 2005 Tech Bulldogs before opening the season at Florida. "You can have the NFL. College is where all the fun is, and trust me, this is the biggest time of your life. Please don't take it for granted. It doesn't get any better than this time in your life."[341]

The football team enjoyed perks, including food and transportation. When the Student Center was built in the '60s, the athletes had a special place below the main floor where they ate in the evenings. Between class and practice hours, players were not able to eat at regular cafeteria hours. Every Friday night, steaks from the campus farm operated by the Department of Agriculture and Forestry were served, individually cooked, along with other farm products such as milk and ice cream. Tech football and most athletic teams rode on a campus bus known as the "Blue Goose," driven by W.L. Sanderson.[342]

Tech's live bulldog mascot, oddly enough, became a mini saga in Coach Aillet's time at Tech. Tech II was run over by a car at El Paso at the 1941 UTEP game. The mascot came from a long line of aristocrats; Tech II's great-great-grandmother was an international winner, selling for $6,500.[343] Other bulldogs served as substitutes for several years. A new live mascot was finally secured in 1948, Aillet being the faculty advisor to the committee who settled on the new bulldog.[344] A tragedy struck again in 1951 when

The new Student Center. *From* The Lagniappe, *1959.*

Tech IX died at two years old due to a heart attack brought on by a heart condition.[345] Early next year, a new live bulldog was found and named Tech X. The bullpup was an escape artist, constantly leaving its pen set up under the bleachers of the stadium, although the tumultuous period of mascot disasters had settled down.[346]

While Coach Aillet's time at Louisiana Tech was the most fulfilling of his coaching career, a few tragedies affected the teams and himself. The Tech coaching staff, going back to the Eddie McLane era, were in several car accidents. While on a trip to Natchitoches in January 1940, the Aillet family suffered a car wreck. A lady driving her children to school pulled out in front of them on Highway 167 between Ruston and Jonesboro. While Bobby and Cynthia, who were in the back of the car, were uninjured, Ruby and little Dickie were thrown against the windshield and received several cuts.[347] Athletic trainer Glenn Tilley was involved in a car accident in the spring of 1957 but made it out all right.[348] Coach Doherty was involved in a car accident in 1960.[349] Thankfully, his was not as serious as previous car accidents.

Left: The ill-fated Tech IX. *From* The Lagniappe, *1949.*

Right: Tech X. *From* The Lagniappe, *1952.*

Great tragedy struck the Aillet family in the 1941 offseason. Dickie Aillet, almost four years old, passed away in his sleep from leukemia after a five-month period of illness. Like other members of the Aillet family, he would be buried at St. Anne's in Youngsville. Pallbearers were all former players of Coach Aillet: Witt Viscocu, Johnny Perritt, Paul Bonin and Delmar "Dude" Pierce, of Louisiana Poly, and Parker Wiggins and Emmett Cope from his Louisiana Normal days. Cope had returned to his hometown of Haynesville and became the head football coach of his alma mater. The 1941 football team attended the funeral at St. Anne's.[350] Dickie's untimely death would deeply hurt the family. It would also prove to be an ominous foreshadowing for Joe Aillet's later fate.

CHAPTER 10

GROWLS, BARKS AND BITES

oach Aillet's practices were well scripted, with the Cajun coach puffing away at a cigarette while he gave instructions.[351] Interestingly, a team poll in 1954 revealed that forty-two of forty-nine players did not smoke despite no team rule prohibiting smoking.[352] However, the rules of Tech prohibited student smoking. One time, Leo Sanford was walking from Keeny Hall to his dorm smoking a cigarette. Coach Aillet started following at a distance. A nervous wreck, Sanford could only hold the cigarette in front of him. Both men walked on for some time; the coach did not change his pace but made Sanford think hard about his decision.[353]

Coach Aillet did also not have a policy against married men: "They have a job to do both scholastically and athletically and if they can do both and be married, that's fine. The young ladies to whom these boys are married are very thoughtful and realize the problems involved in the boys being married, competing in athletics, and fulfilling scholastic requirements."[354] It was not uncommon to find married players on the team; in fact, eleven of the 1958 players were married. He preferred fewer distractions for his players. "There are too many factors that a coach cannot control. Anything from an abnormal bounce of the football to a married player's family quarrel can change the course of the game."[355]

Coach Aillet was forward thinking in his practices, having a keen ability to find the weaknesses of opponents through film.[356] As far back as his Haynesville days, he used film, becoming widely recognized as the first to use the medium for instruction at the high school level.[357] Practices focused less on scrimmage; players broke off into positions groups where the coaches gave targeted instruction and individual training. Players were also surprised when the trainers gave water to the team, contrary to the lack of water breaks in high school at that time. The trainers wiped their faces with cool towels and had lemonade or ice water to cool off.[358] By game time, players had become well assimilated in their areas. Players sat on the bench on the sidelines in groups according to position. Quarterbacks sat close to Coach Aillet in folding chairs.[359]

Tom Hinton found Coach Aillet's practices better organized than any professional teams he played on. When it came time for players to break off into their positions with the assistant coaches, everyone worked efficiently. At a certain time, everyone came back as a single unit without any thought or hesitation.[360]

Crowds of locals gathered to watch the practices. Dr. Sachs enjoyed the athleticism of the players and found it refreshing to stop by practices on his way home. Sometimes, during a break, Coach Aillet came over and visited with him.[361]

Players worked hard on conditioning. One day, Billy Jack Talton confronted Pat Collins and Richard Ennis, both a year younger than him. "I'm older, I've got a year's experience, I'm bigger than you are, I think my attitude's better than yours, but y'all are whipping my butt in practice! What are you doing?"

They replied, "Aw, we just pump a little iron."

"Don't you know that's going to make your muscles bound?"

"Yeah, and it's whipping your butt every day."[362] Back then, weightlifting was thought to tighten athletes' muscles and was not encouraged. The three used space at the old gym across the street from Memorial Gym. Weightlifting became a lifelong hobby for Talton.

Another example of Coach Aillet's methodic approach to coaching was instructing Pat Garrett on his running. Commenting during football practice, he pointed out that he was over-striding and not getting the benefit of the initial short steps required to build up speed. During the transition from the split T to the winged T, Coach Aillet converted Garrett from halfback to quarterback. Garrett did not have the success in college football that he had in high school and was redirected by Coach Aillet into track. Although meeting with Coach Aillet in his office was painful and a letdown, Garrett realized that Aillet was right—he was small by college ball standards, and his track career would serve him better if he concentrated on that.[363]

The coaching staff remained committed to the team's academic performance. Several players struggled academically. Coach Aillet and the coaching staff always tried their best to prevent them from dropping out.[364] Practice started at 4:45 p.m. because labs ran from 1:30 p.m. to 4:30 p.m. School was more important than football, and Coach Aillet scheduled around classes. Such care and attention is not typical, running counter to many football programs at all levels.[365]

At times, as in 1940, academics were a team issue. The enthusiastic team continued to grow, with twenty-six high schoolers hailing from Louisiana and south Arkansas committed for the next season, almost half of whom played in the Louisiana High School All-Star Game.[366] At the same time, however, some players were academically shaky. Aillet wished for faculty "to have a tolerant feeling…with respect to their academic work."[367] Marital commitments, inadequate living facilities in the varsity athletic dorms and injuries sustained in practice plagued the new coach as the season approached. Furthermore, the team as a whole was inexperienced.[368]

J.W. Slack remembered taking a knee during practice, listening to a typical Coach Aillet lecture, watching the other positions running around or hitting one another; times like that made the backfield thankful to rest but they didn't rub it in too hard on the others.[369]

Practice was no cake walk and could be as brutal at Tech as elsewhere. Joe Raymond Peace received a hard hit in practice. A little dazed, the linebacker went into the offensive huddle. Characteristic of Coach Aillet, he said, "Oh Joe, you're in the wrong huddle."[370] There was no fuss—no voices raised, only calmness and firmness.

Lesser hits in practice came from Coach Doherty, who recruited Bill Jones. "Back in those days, the coaches' caps had those metal buttons on top. Well, whenever Coach Doherty wanted to make sure you pushed yourself just a little harder, he'd pop you on the helmet with that cap. I can still hear my helmet ringing when that metal button hit it."[371]

One of the most violent practice incidents occurred when they were running a punt-block drill. A dissatisfied Coach Aillet evidently individually told Max Rudd and C.D. Hart that they needed better effort and would run the play again. The previous play, Hart had almost blocked the punt. Talton was kneeling off to the side with teammates from Minden. They knew enough about fellow Minden teammate Rudd to know that someone was going to be seriously hurt. The next play, Hart gave a wild charge and was met by a Rudd forearm. The devastating blow sent Hart to the ground, bleeding in the mouth. "Oh Glenn," Aillet called to the team trainer, "Check his dental structure."

Left: Aillet in practice gear. *From* The Lagniappe, *1950.*

Below: Practice, 1960. *From* The Lagniappe.

"Dental structure?" thought Talton. "Hell, what dental structure? It's all gone!"[372]

Punting drills were not always as rough. Coach Aillet told A.L. Williams when practicing punts, "When you catch the ball, that's the most important thing you can do is catch it."

"That ain't no problem," thought Williams. "I've already seen that."

Coach continued, "I want you to come and help us. We're going to have a right return. We'll have a right and a left return." This was new to Williams, who had only known to catch the ball where he was and simply find a place to go. "I want you to come up at a certain point. You're going to have to use your common sense and you'll have to feel that. When you hit that certain point, I want you to make a break and I want you to come back in here. Now you'll have to give a little bit, you're going to have to try to get by one or two players. We're going to attempt to block them, but it's hard to block them on a punt return and not hold your block. Everyone's trying to get downfield too. If you can get up to a certain point here and give a little back, we're going to have a wall. If you get to that wall, we'll take you all the way." After practicing that move every day, Williams executed in a scrimmage for a 67-yard touchdown. Again, they signaled for a right return on another punt, and he took it 80 yards for a score. Coach Aillet the next week said, "The first thing you got to do is judge that guy coming at you. They're going to have two head-hunters on each side. They're going to be some of their fastest people—*bad* tacklers. It's going to be hard to hold them back. You got to catch your football first."[373] Against Mississippi Southern, he did as had been instructed, looking up after catching the ball and thought he had plenty of time. His headgear went back on impact, as he was lucky to hold on to the football.

Tom Hinton gained a reputation as a force to be reckoned with. In one instance in 1954, a fellow freshman tackle told Coach Aillet after practice one day, "This college football is a lot tougher than back in high school. In scrimmage yesterday we were told to go half speed. I was opposite Tommy Hinton, and if he was going at half speed I don't want to be around when he's going full speed."[374] That was the last of that particular player on the Tech team.

The Hinton brothers, Pat and Tom, were appreciated, although their brotherly competition was rough. Going up against his younger brother Joe in blocking exercises, Tom was unprepared when Joe hit him hard. "Oh my," exclaimed one of the coaches. "That was a good-looking play. Let's run it again!" Coach Aillet replied, "No, we don't want to run that

Tech attempting to run the ball on Mississippi Southern. *From* The Lagniappe, *1959.*

again."[375] No one wanted to witness two of Tech's finest athletes possibly take each other out.

Before a fateful game with Mississippi Southern, Coach Aillet wanted his defense to practice against the pass. For the first time in his life, Billy Jack Talton had to practice catching the ball, missing numerous passes before he finally caught one. The experience so unnerved him that he tried running over his good friend Mickey Slaughter before being restrained by teammates. The strategy paid off; Talton picked off the Mississippi team late in the game. "Billy Jack," Coach Aillet said, "you catch the ones that count."[376] Praise from the head coach restored his bruised pride.

Bill Jones worked the scout squad as a quarterback, or "practicing dummy." Sometimes, they would show up the varsity team, much to the delight of future Dallas Cowboys coach Jimmy Johnson. Louisiana Tech was Johnson's first coaching job while a graduate assistant in 1965.[377]

When George Doherty had a severe heart attack, he was unavailable for the upcoming season (he was expected to fully recover in a few months). "George is the victim of a great amount of dedication," Coach Aillet said. "He has been under great pressure and has carried a tremendous load for us for years."[378] Coach Aillet was friends with Frank Broyles, accomplished coach of the Arkansas Razorbacks. The two men not only golfed together, but they also traded grad assistants between each other. Johnson took Doherty's place as a defensive coach.[379]

Joe Aillet stories abound. Once, when a storm came up just before practice, it was raining so hard that Mitchell dorm, directly across the field on the other side of Tech Drive, was not visible. As Coach Aillet and Glenn Tilley walked up the hill from Tech Drive, all around the practice field was a downpour, but not a drop fell on the field itself. Glenn Murphy became convinced, as were other players, that Coach Aillet must have had a good relationship with God.[380]

Coach Aillet once told A.L. Williams, "Athletes are like racehorses. The best ones come in with lots of energy. It's a matter of channeling that energy to become productive." This was certainly the case for some of his athletes at Tech, especially one.

It was a rare occasion that Coach Aillet kicked a player off the team for disciplinary issues. One big and strong player had a temper, almost always getting into it with teammates. Even when he didn't physically fight, teammates had to physically step in between him and the other to prevent a fight. "We're here to play football," Coach Aillet said. "You've got to control your temper. I respect your ability to take care of yourself, but that's not why we're here. You're going to have to quit that."

He said, "Yes, sir, I'm sorry about that."

Coach Aillet reminded him after another close call: "The next time, you just got to go. You're disrupting everything." This behavior continued. Finally, after a few seasons, Aillet's patience was exhausted. "Buddy, I'm sorry, but we can't have it. You're going to have to find another place to play." Buddy went to Dr. Sachs, looking for help. "You're going to have to tell me what to do, how to approach him. I can't be kicked off." Dr. Sachs said, "I don't think you have a choice, Buddy. This has been talked about."[381]

Despite cutting the player, Coach Aillet tried to help him by contacting Bud Wilkinson at the University of Oklahoma to let him know he had a really good player who had been released. He warned him that the player was a handful. "I don't care how he is," said Wilkinson. "If he's as good as you say he is we'll make a fine player out of him." A few months later, he called back: "What kind of animal did you send me!" Buddy had returned to his old ways.[382]

Fans across North Louisiana were passionate for the Bulldogs and tried various strategies to ensure a win. In 1953, Gabe Durham, a star player from the early 1930s at Tech, gave the football team an amulet, a mule shoe taken from "the meanest mule in Jackson Parish."[383]

Always wanting the inside scoop, fans were just as excited to hear Coach Aillet explain the game in Ruston as they were in Haynesville. The Quarterback Club was an informal gathering of male sports fans at either Phil's Steak House or Trinity Methodist Church. Women were just as interested in learning more about the game leading up to the State Fair Game, and fifty-three women showed up at the first women's meeting in

1953.[384] "This borders on the fantastic," said Coach Aillet at the opening of the Ladies' Quarterback Club.

A win was a win, regardless of the competition. Before players took showers postgame, there was Coach Aillet, congratulating them. If a player had a good game, they could be excused from Monday practice.[385]

One reason Coach Aillet commanded such respect and loyalty from his athletes was his fairness. He never wavered. He kept his word. If he told a player he would play, even if he wasn't scheduled, he would play. His word was considered the gospel truth.[386]

The Aillet family never missed a game. Yet the 1945 Lake Charles Army Air Base game was difficult to watch, even when Tech won 7–2. Bobby Aillet suffered a broken bone just above the right ankle. Having been hurt in practice earlier in the week, he became seriously injured in a pileup early in the game.[387] Ruby and Cynthia were well aware of Joe's instructions on how to behave at games. Because of his position, they were not to sit in a prominent spot in the stands. If fans responded negatively to a call or play or said anything mean about the coaches, they were not to respond. Therefore, as Bobby was being helped off the field, they remained silent and, as much as possible under the circumstances, dignified. Cynthia later visited her brother in the hospital, unbeknownst to her parents.[388]

Bobby Aillet would join the Naval Academy the next year. Two years later, he was back in Ruston for many reasons: from football, being closer to friends and family—and a sweetheart too. He played a key role in the twilight years of the '40s and wasted little time, marrying his college sweetheart, Dorothy Adams, after the football season.[389]

Football was rough in those days. During one game against McNeese, Billy Jack Talton was punched in the nose. Against Southwestern, Talton lost his poise when he got in a fight with the punter. Talton blocked the punter, who tried in vain to join the chase of the ball carrier, only to be knocked down several times by Talton. Soon, he got up swinging. Talton ducked and hit him again before trying to get him to stop, but it was no use. "I don't have the proper respect for punters," said Talton, "except for David Lee, I like him."[390] Lee was one of Tech's greatest punters, playing in the '60s.

Don Tippit remembered Northwestern State as the team that he least liked losing to, although there was one Arkansas State game that stood out. "We were the better team, but they had two referees on their team, and it was a lousy officiating game. And we lost. Well, Coach Aillet told that head referee after the game, 'You know, usually I get kissed when I get screwed.' And we did, we got a screwing."[391]

The 1966 Alabama game, in Coach Aillet's last year, was also memorable. After the game, Coach Lewis, going to the bus station to pick up film, saw Coach Aillet walking in at the same time. Coach Lewis pulled him to the side, telling him, "We need to find some players that can beat Alabama." "I tell you what you do," he responded. "You take the personnel you got and coach them up."[392]

Coach Mize, in recounting the game, said, "We could almost play with them with our first team. But when they put in their subs and we put in our subs, people started getting tired, it [was] all over. They had 60 guys that were equivalent to Tech's first 20 guys." Paul Bryant also said, "That's the finest passing attack I've ever faced."[393]

The Alabama game had an interesting way of materializing. The Bear, in his autobiography *Bear*, recounted the game in 1976 that made $175,000 when they played USC in 1970. This was not even the biggest moneymaker the Crimson Tide had participated in. The 1966 game against Louisiana Tech was a sellout, with thousands more trying to enter the stadium. After the scheduled Tulane game was scratched, 'Bama was having "a devil of a time getting a game." After bumping the opening game with Southern Miss, Bryant arranged to host the Bulldogs. "I got their athletic director, Joe Aillet, to agree to juggle his schedule around, and when we got down to money, I said, 'Joe, tell me what you want.' He said, 'Shoot, I don't know, Bear, the most we ever made was $15,000.'" After the cash boon from the sellout, Bryant felt guilty and told the athletic board to give an additional $10,000 to Tech. President Taylor also remembered the payout: "After the game was over, Bear Bryant came up to me and said, 'We're going to sweeten your kitty.'"[394] Not to be outdone, the Southern Miss coach called; noting the additional $10,000 sent to the Bulldogs, he pointed out that they were the reason the game was played and wanted compensation, so the Mississippians got $10,000. "It was a matter of numbers," continued Bryant. "If Tech had had the same number of quality players, I wouldn't have wanted to play them. Coach Aillet had done a great job of preparing this team for us.[395] If that guy on the other side of the field had my material, we would have been beaten 100–0."[396]

While Coach Aillet did not like to single games out, he did like the Ole Miss victory in 1946.[397] Another game he remembered well was the 1953 game at Tallahassee against Florida State, the second of two victories against the Seminoles. Coached by Tom Nugent, the Floridians had on their team a freshman, future star Lee Corso. Midway through the game, four well-dressed gentlemen came to the sidelines, asking if it would be all right for

Beginning of the 1966 Alabama game. *From* The Lagniappe.

them to stand there. Coach Aillet told them it was, as long as the police did not object. Later, one of them told him they had never seen a team have so much fun playing football. Aillet was surprised to find that they were four Florida Supreme Court justices.[398]

Tom Causey appreciated Coach Aillet turning him loose against Northeast Louisiana, as he was from Monroe. It was a source of pride to perform well against his hometown. Most notably, Causey remembered being down against Northeast until late in the game, when he was able to slip past the defenders and catch a wounded duck from his friend Mickey Slaughter to win the game. "Coach Aillet was good at putting you in position to excel," he said.[399]

The 1958 McNeese game was special in several respects. The 17–0 Bulldog victory would mark the 100th victory as the Louisiana Tech head coach of Joe Aillet. Previously, he stood at 99-56-8, with a win percentage of .632.[400]

Bud McMichael kicking a field goal in the 1958 McNeese game. *From* the Lagniappe 213.

The best memory Wallace Martin had of playing at Tech was against Mississippi Southern. Scoring the only touchdown in the 10–0 contest on a punt return, Tech won against the hated rivals in part due to Martin's blocking. Shortly before Ken Tidwell ran in for a touchdown, Martin secured a block before looking up to see Ken get tackled in the end zone.[401]

Pat Collins remembered playing against a lineman on the Mississippi Southern team who was quite an athlete and competitor. Above all, he loved to talk trash. When Tech lined up, he was on one knee at the line and told Collins, "Hey, little man. Looks like it's me and you. And when I get over, it's going to be all me." This man, described by Collins as an animal, was enormous, his helmet hardly squeezing over his head. Having choice words in response, Collins took his position. The play was a sweep in which he pulled from his left guard position to block on the right. After the play was over, resulting in a 3- to 5-yard gain, the center Billy Ware stopped him while going back to the huddle. "Collins, you keep your mouth shut. That guy almost killed me!" When Collins pulled, Ware had to reach across his left side to block tackle George "Man Mountain" Hultz.[402] Hultz would later, appropriately, become a professional wrestler.

The 1964 game with Mississippi Southern was lost 14–7, the only team that beat Tech that year. Three years later, Richie Golmon walked into the

Tidwell returning a punt for a touchdown against Mississippi Southern. *From* The Lagniappe, *1963.*

coaches' office in Memorial Gym to find Maxie Lambright, the new head coach. Lambright asked him about the series against Mississippi Southern, the coaches' former team, where the referees controversially ruled several no goal line touchdowns against him in one drive. "Did you think you scored?"

"Yes," replied Golmon.

"I *know* you scored," smiled Lambright.[403]

Joe Hazlip remembered the last game against Southwestern in 1944 during World War II, one of only two times the two schools played each other more than once in the same year. "We had lost to them up here and our last game was in Lafayette. I can recall that Tech had no bus that year, and we borrowed Grambling's bus to get to Lafayette. I can remember that it was a miserable night, very wet. In fact, it was so sloppy and muddy that we took our showers after the game in our uniforms." Robert "Racer" Holstead recalled that "things were pretty unsettled. With guys coming in and out, it was hard to get much consistency."[404] Wingback Johnny Stewart scored the single touchdown of the game, with V.R. Dalrymple making the extra point in the 7–0 victory. The Tech Bluejackets, a spirit group, were present at the hard-fought road victory, a feat the team appreciated because of the transportation challenges of the times.[405]

Gene Knecht remembered one State Fair Game where he was desperately thrown over the goal line. Knecht was on the tail end of a long stretch of Bulldog-dominated victories from 1946 to 1952.[406]

The 1953 SFG illustrates what could happen when gods collide with titans in colossal combat on par with the LSU–Ole Miss or Texas A&M–Texas rivalries of old. James "Red" McNew of Northwestern remembered Pat "Gravy" Patterson and Milford Andrews from their high school days, the Bulldogs being from Delhi and McNew being from Ferriday. Russell Rainbolt was also a great competitor: "Me and Russell ran together head-on quite a few times. I played in the defensive backfield, and Russell was a good runner, the hardest runner I ever tackled. He was a real determined runner, and he was a good-sized runner. A.L. Williams was a good runner, but Rainbolt at 190 pounds was a little bigger, and for a guy who weighed 160 pounds...to come up and tackle him, it was a lot of work."[407]

The SFG was the biggest grudge match for Tech, bigger than Southwestern or Southern Miss. There was never a good time to lose to the Demons. A.L. Williams recalled the 1953 loss. "I remember how disappointed I was and how unusual Coach Aillet handled it. It certainly was a bitter loss for him. He said very quietly, 'You had a nice game, son.' He said very little. All my time at Tech I can remember that freshman year. It was a very, very dark Monday, it looked like it was going to storm. Coach Mize referred to it as 'Black Monday.'"[408]

Everyone was quiet on the bus home until one player yelled out the window to a friend, finalizing meetup plans for a dance. Everyone else cringed. When they got back to Ruston, Coach Aillet brought them onto the field as he addressed them on one knee. "I think we need to have a little talk. It seems that everyone was thinking about the dance after the game. That was evident during the game. We're going to see if we can't get our minds on football for a while. Before we do that, we'll need some changes."

The ensuing practice on Black Monday saw almost everyone switch to new positions, Aillet coaching almost every position. Before long, one of the centers broke a leg. Russell Rainbolt injured his knee. Williams, who was on defense at the moment, took Rainbolt's spot and never gained a yard the entire practice. "As long as he was here, I'd never seen a scrimmage like that."

"For Coach Aillet, probably not so much the winning of the State Fair Game was the fact that should we have lost one," observed Coach Mize. "The following week was a terrific lesson in hard football at Tech practices. When you lost to Northwestern, everybody walked lightly around the Tech athletic office. You walked like you walk on cotton. Very quietly."

Gayle Dick running up the middle in the 1953 State Fair Game; notice the servicemen in attendance. *From* The Lagniappe.

McNew had a different recollection of the '53 game. "It was always an upset when we beat them because they always had a decided advantage on us. Kind of exciting. They declared it a holiday. Monday, everybody got out of class for a big pep rally. It was quite a deal."

Other Tech players making a mark on McNew's memory were the Hinton brothers. "For the '50s, they were as big as the linemen are now. They were unusually big for our conference." McNew did not have fond memories of the 1955 SFG. "I got hurt on the opening kickoff...got my knee messed up. One of the Hintons slid in behind the blocking, turned me upside down. Just came in, about 230 pounds, got me on the side. But I played the entire game. Drug my leg around the rest of the game."

This time, Williams would have the last laugh. After scoring a touchdown, he had to kick the extra point. Rules at that time curtailed substitutions; since the two regular kickers were out, he had to kick. Remembering the fateful conversion and winning 10–8, "It came out in the paper that when the pressure was on, Coach Aillet knew who to call on to kick the extra point. What really happened, someone on our sideline was really getting on me. They said, 'Oh, no, not him.'"[409]

The State Fair Game typically brought out the worst in student behavior; it comes with the territory in rivalries. However, in 1964 George W. D'Artois, commissioner of public safety in Shreveport, sent a letter to President Taylor congratulating him on the Bulldog victory: "We had a nice experience when the students of Louisiana Tech were guests in Shreveport for the fair and to attend the Louisiana Tech–Northwestern game. The students were well-behaved and depicted a spirit of cultural training which bespeaks credit due the president and all the faculty of Louisiana Tech. Their cooperation with the police officers made each detail so much easier."[410] The next year, Mayor Clyde E. Fant sent a similar letter to Taylor: "Certainly, having the faculty, student body, and many graduates here is an honor to our city."[411]

In Coach Aillet's career at Louisiana Tech, one statistic stands out. Among the many successful seasons, not one bowl game was played. It was not for lack of effort or results. Tech was invited to two bowls in 1948, the Tangerine Bowl, in the second year of its existence, and the Shrine Bowl in Arkansas. Tech refused both invitations, saying that it would prolong the season into late December.[412] Such reasoning would seem odd, especially as there was no further explanation for the refusal. It is not uncommon, though, for teams to pass on bowl invitations then or now.

Tech finished bowl-less in 1959 as well. Even though Tech finished fourth in the AP Poll, fifth in the UPI Poll and first in the Pecan Bowl Poll in 1964, Tech was not invited to play in the bowl.[413] Instead, it would be the last opportunity for an Aillet-coached Louisiana Tech team to enter a bowl.

Coach Aillet's first years at Tech, marked by the Second World War, saw the football team move in a direction that, while still far removed from the modern game, established the base for further innovations. At the time, Aillet played a key role professionally and spiritually by spearheading the formation of the Gulf States Conference and being part of the founding of St. Thomas Aquinas church. Leadership-wise, Aillet came in at a time when the coaching staff was in disarray; results on the gridiron were far below fan expectations, and confidence in the program was low. Aillet could have completely razed the old regime, as is often the case in sports. His coaching abilities and personal appeal would have meant few people would question or protest any actions. Instead, no coaches were forced out. Mike Wells, one of the original Howard College followers of Coach McLane, remained with the team from 1940 to 1945. McLane himself remained at Tech in the Department of Physical Education until retiring in 1966 and being replaced by Garland Gregory.[414] Aillet's gracious manner meant that people wanted to coach with him. Coaches Crowley and Mize were successful championship-winning coaches yet chose to stay with Louisiana Tech and Coach Aillet.

Coach Aillet was able to take a floundering program and turn it into a powerful force in the state. Several of his teams were only a few mistakes away from perfect seasons. What stands out is his development of talent with the first All-Americans of the institution while creating an overall culture of outstanding young men.

Part of this success was the elimination (before the 1942 season) of old traditions such as the Varsity House. Ruby washed towels for the athletes when the Aillets first came to Tech, as they lived close by.[415] The college could not afford the building during wartime, and athletes were dispersed among regular campus dorms.[416] Instead of being segregated from the rest of campus, athletes were integrated with regular dorms. Special treatment of players, almost bordering on awe, ceased. The main reason the athletic dorm was not brought back was because Coach Aillet wanted the players to mingle with the rest of the students instead of closing themselves off.[417] "You're here to make lifelong connections," said Aillet. "How can you do that if you see the same people every day?"[418]

Many former players would return and assist with coaching future teams in various capacities and go on to have successful careers at the high school and college level. Some had success as professional football players; though only spending the 1944 season at Tech in the V-12 program, Cloyce Box had a bright future with the Detroit Lions.[419] While there were some bumps on the way—such as the 1940 Ouachita Baptist defeat, the 1944 season and losses against the key rivals of Northwestern, Southwestern and Mississippi Southern—there were plenty of accomplishments. Only one losing season was incurred during the difficult '40s, several rivalry series were flipped in Tech's favor, SEC teams were beaten and tied and three championships were won. Coach Aillet could have gone to several big southern schools but chose to stay and leave his stamp on the football program of Louisiana Tech and the city of Ruston.

CHAPTER 11

GOLF COACH

C oach Aillet's golfing exploits predated his coaching days. There were the Haynesville years, including the time when he met Jimmy Mize at the Louisiana State Amateur Championship Golf Tournament. Aillet remained competitive with his Ruston friends. Local interest was so high that KRUS radio would occasionally carry the matches live. Sometimes he would leave notes behind for his family in the form of golf balls; when Cynthia would open the door, one would bounce across the floor to let her know that he had been by.[420]

The Cajun coach and Ruby were frequently competitors in regional events and won on occasion. The 1951 golf season would be busier than usual; already the chairwoman of the Ruston Women's Golf Tourney Committee, Ruby was chosen to the board of directors of the newly formed Northeast Louisiana Women's Golf Association. Ruby would immediately play a role in policymaking.[421]

Frequently, Tech was invited to tournaments across the South and usually performed well. Roy Nash, one of the best Tech golfers, won the Louisiana Amateur Meet during the 1958 season, becoming the first Tech player to do so.[422] He lost in a rematch against Burt Burdick in the quarterfinals of the 1959 Louisiana Amateur Meet, having beaten him in the previous year's finals.[423]

Another Roy, Roy Pace, won acclaim at Tech. Before the 1963 golf season began, Pace took honors for his performance at the New Orleans Open. As the top amateur golfer, he won a new golf bag for his efforts.[424] The

Roy Pace showing a golf bag won at the 1958 Louisiana Amateur Golf Meet. *From* The Lagniappe.

golf program as a whole was less successful; before the season, Coach Aillet admitted, "Unless we get help before too long, the caliber of golf here will deteriorate. All the other teams in the conference are improving rapidly."[425]

Some of Tech's best golfers finished their careers in '63, including Pace. "It will be one of our few lean years,"[426] said Coach Aillet. While Tech still won the conference meet in '64, they began a slow decline.

Coach Aillet had a wide degree of success coaching Tech golf. He correctly predicted a championship season in 1941[427] but did not predict that it would be an undefeated one. The first championships in GSC competition came in 1953–57 and again in 1960–64. The last championship, 1969, was well earned and greatly pleased Coach Aillet. One of the golfers on the '69 team got a rare emotional response out of Coach Aillet. Rick Hollan made a birdie from eight feet out to put Tech ahead at the GSC championship, held at the Ruston Country Club. "It was the only time I ever saw him just really break out and laugh," said Hollan. "He wasn't one to let his emotions show outwardly."[428] Other notable seasons included some second-place finishes in 1952, 1958 and 1959 and third-place finishes in 1948 and 1965.

Roy Pace came to Tech in the middle of Coach Aillet's golf reign. Pace would become the only professional golf alumnus of the university and a testament to Coach Aillet's influence. Starting from humble beginnings in the South Texas town of Kenedy, Pace eyed his father's golf clubs at a young age. Like so many other golfers, he got his start by caddying at the local nine-hole golf course. When he wasn't caddying, he was trying to play on his own. He made an improvised green at his house, consisting of a hole in the ground with a tin can. When his family moved to Longview in East Texas, he continued playing and improved his game. North Texas State offered him a scholarship, but his father's friend, a Tech graduate and acquaintance of Aillet's, convinced him to check out Tech because he was interested in mechanical engineering. Meanwhile, Coach Aillet was told, "You ought to have a look at this boy." Pace was invited for a visit; a scholarship offer sealed the deal.

Golf was a sport that allowed Coach Aillet to relax from the strains of the football season. He made careful notes of each player's golf swings. His friendship with fellow Cajuns and professional golfers Jay and Lionel Hebert brought additional resources to Tech to help train his players. As Pace was deciding to turn pro, Jay became a mentor to him and helped him enter the PGA Tour.

While Pace starred at Tech, winning several matches and the individual score three of the four years he competed in collegiate golf, one tournament stuck out in his mind. Qualifying for the New Orleans Open, he beat Arnold Palmer and Jack Nicklaus in the first round of competition while an amateur. They would go on to beat him later in the tournament, but the thrilling experience pointed him in the direction of going pro. Another fond memory of his career was shooting the Ruston Country Club course record at ten under par 62 his senior year.

Pace enjoyed the small college environment and the engineering program, one of the selling points for attending Tech. With quality professors and lifelong friendships made inside and out of golf, he was indebted to Tech. While only using his engineering to work for Bobby Aillet at Aillet, Fenner, Jolly and McClellan one fall, the courses prepared him for his life journey. In that case, both engineering and golf worked well, as he met potential clients and played golf with them. Pace remained in the profession as a teacher of golf and occasionally visits his alma mater to pump up the current golfers, thankful for the lifelong influence of Tech golf and Coach Aillet.[429]

CHAPTER 12

LIFE AFTER FOOTBALL

March 30, 1967, marked the last day of Joe Aillet's coaching career. He spent one year at Southwestern as a student coach, nine years at Haynesville High School (four as an assistant and five as head coach), four years as an assistant at Northwestern State and twenty-six years as head coach at Louisiana Tech. Cited as reasons in the official letter of resignation were the twin roles of athletic director and head football coach, by custom held by one man. Coach Aillet was exhausted, unable to devote enough time to either position or execute their functions at the best of his ability. Therefore, he would focus on athletic director and leave the head coaching position open for new blood. The news was accepted by President Taylor, who officially welcomed Aillet to remain as athletic director.[430]

"You should see what your peers are saying about you now that you've retired from active coaching," said Bill McIntyre of the *Shreveport Times* on the phone. "It may turn your head."

"That's only natural," laughed Aillet. "They hate to see a loser go out… the most gratifying thing in all my career is the close association with the athletes and the members of the coaching staff. I can assure you the rewards of coaching are not financial. It's the good will of the boys themselves. Stepping out of active coaching takes the core out of my existence."[431]

Praise was quick and widespread for the retired coach, from those involved in athletics to fans and those not directly involved in athletics. The Louisiana Tech Chapter of the American Association of University Professors commended his time at Tech.[432] As for the coaches and administrators of the GSC, they were in shock.[433] All had to collect their thoughts, reflecting on their long professional relationships with Aillet: Dixie White of Northeast and Jack Rowan, formerly of Northeast; Jack Clayton of Northwestern State and Glenn Gossett, soon-to-be head coach of Northwestern State; Russ Faulkenberry and Pat Kennelly of Southeastern, as well as E.L. "Ned" McGehee, athletic director of Southeastern; Jim Clark of McNeese State and Les DeVall, formerly of McNeese State; Bill Allgood, athletic director of Louisiana College; and Stan Galloway, commissioner of the GSC.

The prior year also saw a reconciliation between two parties that had declared war on each other almost a decade prior. Wiley Hilburn Jr. had incurred criticism from Coach Aillet at the end of the '59 9-1 championship season for the lack of a bowl game.

Oddly enough, both Memphis State and Mississippi Southern finished the season ranked ahead of Louisiana Tech despite Tech victories over them. Hilburn put forth several reasons, generating a substantial degree of annoyance. The rankings took place before the last game of the season between Tech and Southern. Size and competition-wise, Tech was small and played small competitors. The Gulf States Conference only contained small Louisiana schools. While these were valid complaints, it could also be that since it was Tech's first real public, attention-grabbing football season outside the region and outside the South, sportswriters and committee members on a national scale did not know how to properly consider the team. After all, playing such highly ranked schools as Lamar Tech, Memphis State and Mississippi Southern and only losing a close game to one while blowing out the other two was evidence of the power possessed by the players and the preparation, foresight and execution of the coaching staff. Sharing his thoughts on the postseason ranking fiasco, Coach Aillet said, "With the proper athletic publicity, we could have been number one."[434] Regardless, the legendary season produced an uproar among some sections of the college town and would lead to a general belief that Tech was capable of more beyond its "small college play" that had characterized it up until now. The consequences of this would be far-reaching down into the present day and would eventually overtake Coach Aillet, the man who played perhaps the largest role in getting Tech to such a stage.

Having felt that Aillet's criticism was undue, Hilburn, working for *The Tech Talk* and *Daily Leader*, responded to the effect that if the engineering program at Tech could become nationally known, the football team could too. These would be fighting words for any coach, let alone someone who *was* nationally known, even if the football program was not. The feud started with a fiery speech at a Rotary Club meeting, resulting in Hilburn being banned for a year from the press box. Hilburn Sr. got involved, threatening to "whip his [Coach Aillet's] ---."

The feud ended in 1966 when Hilburn interviewed Aillet and Paul Bryant for the *Shreveport Times* in anticipation of the Alabama game. Coach Aillet told him that the game was not because of the articles he had written and showed him multiple letters from teams across the country that were afraid to play his Bulldogs as evidence to the difficulty of scheduling prime competition. The two made up and remained close friends for years to come.[435]

Taking his place as head football coach was Maxie Lambright. Hailing from Southern Miss, Lambright quarterbacked from 1946 to 1948, graduating in 1949, and then accumulated eighteen years as a football coach. He found success in coaching, first as an assistant coach at Greenwood and Greenville High Schools and as head coach of Winona High School in Mississippi before coaching at Bolton High in Alexandria, Louisiana. Lambright had been on the coaching staff at Southern Miss since 1959; Tech would be his first and only head coaching position in college football, like Aillet. "Louisiana Tech is indeed fortunate to secure the services of such a splendid coach as Maxie Lambright," said President Taylor. "He is a winner and a gentleman, and I am confident that he will continue the same great tradition in football which Louisiana Tech has enjoyed for so long under Joe Aillet."[436]

Lambright would craft a coaching staff that included mostly former players from the Aillet era and initially retained a few coaches from his staff. Mize remained on the team until later focusing solely on track and field, while Lewis remained on the football team for several years. Mickey Slaughter, Pat Collins and Pat Patterson were called back, Slaughter from the Denver Broncos and Collins and Patterson from high school coaching ranks. Patterson, an end who played in the early '50s, would become better known for his baseball coaching, becoming the namesake of Pat Patterson Park. He replaced longtime coach Berry Hinton. The only non-Bulldog on the staff, outside the head coach, was Tony Misita, a defensive line coach from Southeastern. Wallace Martin joined in 1971 when Misita left for Tulane.

The new coaching staff was not the Aillet staff. Intensity, noise and profanity were amped up. Previously, Doherty and Lewis had been the most animated on the Aillet staffs, although there was rarely if ever any foul language—Coach Aillet would not have allowed it. Misita became so impassioned before games that he often threw up during the pregame. Lambright could also be hard at times; while always open to new ideas from his coaching staff, such as switching from the option offense he was accustomed to back to the pro-style offense previously ran by Aillet, he let it be known when his final decision was made and could become rough with the staff and players. One day, what was supposed to be an offense versus defense drill turned into a scrimmage. As it was against the plans for the day, Coach Lambright was far from pleased. Slaughter and Collins, the ones responsible for the amplification of the drills, earned his wrath. "He charged up that hill and he was yelling, really giving it to us," said Slaughter. "All we could do was keep our mouths shut," as Lambright continued to dog them after practice. "You had to steel your mind that you were going to get your butt chewed out once or twice a day."[437]

Despite the shift in coaching styles, the Bulldogs would replicate the success of the Aillet era. After a difficult 3-7 1967 season, Tech reached new heights, going to their first bowl games in school history and registering an undefeated 1972 season. Ushered in by Lambright was the beginning of the "big-time ball play" that had been pushed for several years. Athletes who played at the tail-end of Aillet's career saw success with Lambright as well. Bobby Brunet, Terry Bradshaw and Tommy Spinks would play professionally, for the Washington Redskins, the Steelers and the Minnesota Vikings, respectively.

While remaining the golf coach, Aillet was busy as athletic director and occasionally took on other leadership roles. He became part of the selection committee for the Grantland Rice Bowl in 1968.[438] For two years, the Bulldogs made it to the Grantland Rice Bowl, winning in '68 over Akron and losing in '69 against East Tennessee State. As Tech celebrated one hundred years of college football with the rest of the country, Coach Aillet said, "We at Louisiana Tech feel it will always play an integral part in college life and in our entire society. There is certainly a need for competitiveness and discipline within the structure of our nation and college football aids greatly in development of these traits."[439] Louisiana Tech participated in sixty-six of those one hundred years of football.

Phil Robertson, Coach Aillet's last lead quarterback, did not last long after Coach Aillet retired from football. Bradshaw, having shared playing time with Robertson, would take his place. Robertson's best game was the 1966 Alabama game. If Aillet had stayed on a few more years, he would have retained Robertson. As late as February 1967, one month before he retired, he had words of praise for his quarterback: "His attitude for the job is perfect, his footwork is flawless, and his passing has looked better than ever before."[440] Instead, Robertson ceded the starting position to

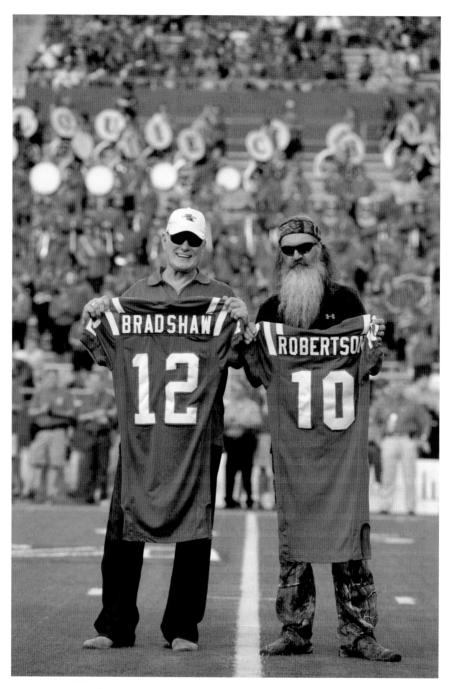

Terry Bradshaw and Phil Robertson receive jerseys with their numbers from their playing days at Tech. *From the Louisiana Tech Sports Communication Department.*

Terry Bradshaw, one becoming an NFL Hall of Famer and the other the "Duck Commander."

Bradshaw was a much-anticipated draft pick in 1970. Among the many compliments he received, Coach Aillet reflected on recruiting the Shreveport talent: "Bradshaw was a good passer in high school and Baylor and LSU were both interested in him. I think the main reason we got him is that we are a pro set team, and he is a drop back passer. He still has a tremendous potential to be developed when he learns more about defenses."[441]

Coach Aillet also noted that Bradshaw was giving up javelin in track in order not to jeopardize his throwing arm. Bradshaw became the first small college player to earn the top selection in the NFL and remains the only Louisiana Tech player to become the first overall pick in a professional sports league draft.

Aillet kept up with the sports world outside of the GSC. He correctly pointed to a rising star at LSU. When talking to Bud Montet of the *Baton Rouge Morning Advocate* about the quarterback position in 1971, Montet was describing how upset everyone was in Tiger Town that they missed out on Joe Ferguson to Arkansas. "You know, Montet, this boy Jones just might make LSU a better quarterback than Ferguson. He's the Tigers' type of player and I think he'll make it good."[442] Of course, he knew the family of Bert Jones well and was very aware of the Ruston Rifle's talent.

Life as athletic director was often far from ideal, however. While Coach Aillet anxiously awaited the completion of the new athletic facilities, he experienced varying degrees of both pressure and neglect emanating from the highest office at the college. One day, Coach Aillet came home from work and asked his daughter if he was invisible. "I see every bit of you," Cynthia told him. "Are you being treated as if you're not there?"

"I think you could say that,"[443] he said.

The year 1970 was the start of one of Aillet's roughest times in his life. Having asked to remain as athletic director until the soon-to-be completion of the stadium, the request was turned down. The request was sent directly to President Taylor, who in turn delivered it to the State Board of Education. The mandatory retirement age for his position stood at sixty-five. President Taylor objected to the request because of the mandatory retirement age, and the board agreed, although the decision was not immediately published. The policy had gone into effect July 1, 1967, shortly after Coach Aillet's retirement from football.[444] President Taylor proceeded to recommend Maxie Lambright to replace Aillet. No one, neither Coach Aillet nor the Athletic Committee, knew of the decision until it was announced a few weeks later. Coach Aillet only found out while at the McNeese golf tournament.[445] Almost immediately after his forced retirement, Tech left the Gulf States Conference, the organization whose development was largely spearheaded by Aillet, to join the Southland Conference.

A rally of support for the veteran coach resulted in a second Joe Aillet Day, held at the Student Center. Aillet pointed to the fact that more than 90 percent of his players earned their degrees; he was especially proud of the many who entered business and coaching careers, seeing their successes as his life work. Reflecting on the initial struggle to turn the Bulldog program around, he said, "The first thing we did at Tech was put in some academic requirements for the boys on scholarship. We lost 21 boys off the squad because of that and went into that first season somewhat depleted, but we were going into the right direction in the academic area."

One of the many years he recounted was the 1945 season; due to the war, most of the team were freshmen, mere seventeen- to eighteen-year-olds, and they still managed a 6-4 record. The 1946 team included several veterans returning from war. "They really enjoyed football because they had been to war and how could football be a matter of life and death to them after having been in action? So, they had fun and, while there were reports all over the nation about trouble from ex-servicemen, we had none here."

Team composition again returned to the North Louisiana region in 1947. "We had established ourselves in the welfare of our athletes. They were getting their degrees and playing winning football and the high school coaches were interested in that for their kids. So, we were able to maintain good contacts and we used the recommendations of the high school coaches in doing our recruiting."[446]

"I do not know of a more rewarding profession than coaching football," Coach Aillet said. "If I had to live my life over, I would do the same thing. I wouldn't want to avoid any of the troubles I have encountered in the past."[447] Aillet was not just a football coach but also a teacher. "I've always enjoyed teaching, whether in the classroom or on the football field or golf course,"[448] he said.

While at Southwestern, Coach Aillet taught commerce, and while at Northwestern, he taught accounting and earned a master's in history and commerce.[449] He graduated from LSU with his master's in 1937, with his thesis titled "The History of Education in Claiborne Parish."[450] His experience as a teacher, from history to civics, mathematics and bookkeeping and as a coach at Haynesville, also affected the philosophy that he used at Tech. "I've always considered coaching football and golf as a teaching experience. Athletics are a tremendous field in which to learn how to live—all experiences teach you something about how to live life." Unfortunately for Aillet, his enormous duties at Tech only allowed him one class to teach: "The Theory of Football."

One compliment he received in 1932 while at Haynesville stayed in his mind the most. T.H. Harris, once the state superintendent, was visiting the school in his native Claiborne Parish. After being able to follow what Coach Aillet was doing in his practice by scanning his clipboard, Harris became impressed and told him if all the teachers in the state followed the same procedures in classes, many education problems would be solved.

Comparing athletics to banking, medical, legal and retail professions, Coach Aillet cautioned, "Each case depends upon what you do with it—it can be tremendous, or it can be lousy or even destructive."[451] In his opinion, there was becoming too much of an emphasis on winning. "Winning cannot be the objective of every coach. Somebody has got to lose. I always wanted to win because winning is the mark of a successful venture, but you have to lose sometimes."

At the same time, he thanked the passionate Bulldog fans. "While I was at Tech, the alumni and fans in general paid me the compliment that I had the right to lose. They knew we wouldn't accept defeat, but they were mature and vitally interested in my program and realized that we couldn't win every time."

Much about sports that he had grown up with and worked in was changing. Aside from the development of wide receivers to spread the field

Original SFG pennant. *From* The Lagniappe, *1951.*

Above: Dancing President Ropp joins cheerleaders in pregame rally before the 1959 SFG; the band and homecoming court are in the background, while the hospitality group known as the Bluejackets are facing the performance. *From* The Lagniappe.

Opposite, top: Tech faithful at a rainy 1959 homecoming game; notice the smokestack from the university power plant behind the stadium. *From* The Lagniappe.

Opposite, bottom: Shortly before the 1965 homecoming game against Southwestern. *From* The Lagniappe.

and a continuation of triple option play and defensive adjustments to these innovations, he believed that the present athletes were different from those of the past. They were more sophisticated, wanted to do more on their own, traveled more frequently and over longer distances and were using weights more. The most pronounced concerns he had revolved around coaching: "Today, the true values of football are being set aside by many coaches for the sake of publicity, personal gain, or self-promotion. This gets them away

Tech XI and Tech XII inspect the campus. *From* The Lagniappe, *1961.*

from the true objective of the system: helping the boys. This has gotten out of hand, and we can't do anything about it. The coaches will go along with the trend because they have families to take care of."[452]

Wishing to show their support for the coach in this unpleasant ending to his decades of service to the institution, coaches across the nation sent telegrams. Paul Bryant, Johnny Vaught, Frank Broyles, Tom Landry, Blanton Collier, Ralph Jordan, Tom Fears, Jim Pittman and Ray Graves sent their congratulations on the conclusion of his coaching career. Former players and those who knew him gave testimony to his influence on their lives to the four-hundred-person audience.[453]

Former players Caleb Martin, Mike Reed, A.L. Williams and Leo Sanford spoke of his coaching ability, character and impact on their lives. Players of all the decades were there, such as Ken Liberto, Terry Bradshaw, Tommy Spinks and Larry Brewer, who came to Tech before Aillet retired and played after he left. Harry Turpin, his old superior at Northwestern State, also spoke highly of him, as did as his former assistant coaches George Doherty, now an assistant coach at Northwestern State, and Jimmy Mize. Several former coaches who coached against him in the GSC were there, such as Glenn Gossett, Jack Clayton, Dixie White and Jack Rowan. Eddie Robinson of Grambling also came to wish him well.

Russ Faulkinberry, head coach of Southwestern, recalled the first Joe Aillet Day back at the Tech homecoming of '63 when his Ragin' Cajuns were crushed, 45–0. Hazel Rogers, one of his secretaries, was thankful for having him as her boss, and Scott Weathersby spoke for the faculty in noting his attention to academics.

Jack Brittain, a former player now working as an attorney, presented his former coach with an oil painting of himself and let it be known that the veteran Bulldog players intended that the new stadium should be named in Aillet's honor. Aillet's son, Bobby, presented him with a gold watch, one of many gifts, including a pendant of Aillet; a bronze etching of himself, for Ruby; a Louisiana Tech blanket; and resolutions from State Commissioner of Athletics Stan Galloway and the Louisiana Tech Alumni Association. "This timepiece signifies the devotion that he gave to young men and to Tech," said Bobby.

"If all of the nice things that have been said about me have any basis, then to you ex-athletes I am indebted," said Coach Aillet. "Through you I have been able to repay my debt to athletics."[454]

Slack's last memory of seeing Coach Aillet was on the second Joe Aillet Day. Coach Aillet was in a wheelchair, recovering from surgery. He sat in the walkway of the new stadium with his mentor, overlooking the field.[455]

The home stadium of Coach Aillet's Tech career had been constructed in 1935. The first game played, beating Southwestern, was the first night game played at Tech. Originally, it held a 5,000-seat capacity before being built up to an additional 3,000 seats.[456] The new 1968 stadium had a capacity of 23,318 seats. In an ambitious and aggressive effort overseen by Joe Aillet, a new all-weather track, tennis courts and baseball field were also built at the same time, along with a fieldhouse.[457]

The last committee Coach Aillet served on selected the All-Decade team of the GSC.[458] Of the Tech players who made the list, all were coached by Aillet—Bradshaw, Spinks, Brewer and Joe Hinton. After all the years of him bestowing honors on players, he would be repaid in kind, receiving plaques from several of the organizations representing sports in Louisiana. The Louisiana Tech Faculty Senate lauded his career in a resolution.[459]

While he appreciated the outpouring of support, Coach Aillet's body began to show signs of trouble. A diagnosis of cancer led to abdominal surgery in 1970.[460] In 1971, he again had surgery.[461] One negative factor to his health was his smoking. "I wish I had never smoked, and I should've quit a long time ago. But the only way that I will ever stop is because I want to quit on my own. Unless I decide myself, I will never stop smoking. I must motivate myself."[462]

New stadium after construction. *From the 1969 Louisiana Tech Football brochure.*

Having tried to set an example for his players, he acknowledged that it had not worked and that a stronger method might be required. Eventually, he became confined to a hospital bed in his home. While at Ochsner's for the last time in 1971, a nurse asked if he needed a psychiatrist, as he was terminally ill. "Indeed not," he said, "I think I got this handled."[463] He wanted to carry on as close to normal as possible; not once did he question God or let himself become a victim. One frequent visitor was Eddie Robinson. On some occasions, Robinson and Aillet and Cynthia, his caregiver, would talk. Other times, when Coach Aillet was too weak to carry a conversation, he would sit there and silently keep him company.

The Tech and Grambling coaches and Grambling president Ralph Waldo Emerson Jones had a friendship of mutual respect and assistance. Poly's Robert "Moose" Phillips drove some Louisiana Negro Normal (now Grambling State University) student organizations to events in the late '30s and early '40s. Moose served as bus driver for most sports teams and campus music groups at Tech as well as Grambling choir.[464] The 1942 campaign had its own problems aside from the war. Due to maintenance issues with the Poly bus, the fairly new 1940 model bus of Grambling was used along with a driver; cost was handled by the football team along with a postseason bouquet of thanks.[465] The Lions Bowl, a charity game for less fortunate children in the Ruston area, was hosted at Tech Stadium and sponsored by the Ruston Lions Club for Grambling to play other Black colleges in the '40s and '50s.[466] Coach Robinson could often be seen watching Tech football practices with other locals, as he did with Hoss Garrett and Ruston High.[467] All three greatly respected one another and the work accomplished in their profession.

On December 28, 1971, Joe Aillet passed away at sixty-seven, a year after his brother Clarence and one week after Tech basketball Hall of Famer Jackie Moreland died of cancer. Both had similar surgeries at Ochsner's Clinic in New Orleans.[468] That same year, the GSC, the conference that was the brainchild of Aillet, was abandoned by the remaining teams.[469] Response was swift among those who were affected, such as former players Joel Thomas, Mike Reed and Leo Sanford, as well as Johnny Perritt, then serving as mayor of Ruston.

Because Aillet was known to help sportswriters give a better picture of the Louisiana Tech football program, several of them also had kind words of remembrance. Ed Shearer, a Tech alumnus and Southeast sports editor for the Associated Press, and Bill Ebarb of *The Tech Talk* were glad to have worked with him. Others recounted interesting stories with Aillet and Tech football. Bobby Henderson, another Tech alumni and sports information director at Southwestern, enjoyed the first plane ride the football team went on in 1948 to play Bradley College in Peoria, Illinois.[470]

Rick Bryan remembered working with Coach Aillet as the sports editor of the *Monroe Morning World* and the *Ruston Daily Leader*. After liking a story Bryan wrote in the *World*, Coach Aillet called him and sent a note in thanks. When he came to Ruston, Coach Aillet talked to him, "Come by my office every week before the game and I'll tell you what we're going to do, then you can watch for it and have something to write the other papers won't have."[471]

Coach Aillet would always respond if Bryan needed help, even after he moved and worked for a magazine; one time, while Aillet was suffering from his illness, he gave himself as a reference over the phone and helped Bryan get a job.

O.K. Buddy Davis, a Tech graduate who would for decades work as the sports editor of the *Ruston Daily Leader*, remembered the personal moments they shared, such as his fond memories of his St. Edward's days. One of his proudest moments was when Eddie Robinson called him after winning his 200th victory as a Grambling head coach in the past year.[472] "I just wanted to share this with you," said Robinson to Aillet. "It would have been empty of meaning without your helping me celebrate."[473]

Like Bryan, Davis was in touch with Aillet while he was sick, receiving a note of thanks for a piece on Tech football he wrote. "He was an inspiration to all athletes and stood for good sportsmanship," said Harold Smolinski, department head of the Accounting Department at Louisiana Tech and chairman of the Athletic Council. "He wanted all players to excel in their academic work. All his players tried to emulate him in their lives. I know. I played for him and worked with him."[474]

Coaches who were very close to Aillet once again made statements honoring his life, from Eddie Robinson to Stan Galloway, Harry Turpin, Jimmy Mize and George Doherty, as well as Congressman Joe Waggoner, who spoke at the first Joe Aillet Day.

Dr. Sachs's eulogy at the Rotarian Club touched on several aspects of Joe Aillet's life. He recounted a few of the highlights of his coaching career, such as the Alabama game, the all-star players he coached and Coach Robinson visiting him the past year during his sickness. A game from the early '50s stood out in his recollection for the sportsmanship of the old coach. After playing a rough team on the road, Aillet told him that he would have rather lost the game than won it under the circumstances because of the type of game the other team had resorted to. He remembered Aillet the athlete and Aillet the gamer, who excelled with his wife at billiards and bridge. As to Aillet's appreciation for literature, none was as familiar with it as Sachs. On one occasion, he requested individual copies of Shakespeare plays from Sachs so he could read in bed without worrying about a large volume. While many comments had been made on Aillet's courage in the face of his illness, Sachs relayed that the source of his courage primarily came from his religious convictions, which had developed at an early age. Much of the Joe Aillet we know of came from his upbringing back in Youngsville and at Holy Cross in New Orleans.[475]

Coach and Mrs. Robinson paid their respects to a dear friend at the Requiem Mass held in Ruston before the burial at St. Anne's in Youngsville, where the rest of his family was buried. As Coach Robinson talked to Coach Mize afterward, he told him, "I owe a lot to Coach Aillet. I've had a good career and been there many years, but Coach Aillet was here all those years and any time I had a problem, he'd help me out."[476]

Pallbearers were Jimmy Mize, George Doherty, Jack Fiser, Jim Stokes, Harold Smolinski and Dr. J.J. Thigpen.

Two landmarks of Louisiana Tech, the football stadium and fieldhouse, were promptly named Joe Aillet Stadium by President Taylor in accordance with the wishes of the Aillet family.[477] The stadium and fieldhouse, aside from being the most prominent places to assign to Joe Aillet, were the most appropriate. Coach Aillet was responsible for overseeing the development of the stadium, as well as being behind its design. He was always remembered fondly by students; the Student Government Organization passed a proclamation of thanks for his services. The stadium and fieldhouse dedication took place during the homecoming game against Eastern Michigan in 1972; Tech was the second-ranked Division II team at the time and would have an undefeated season, the last such season for a Bulldog team to date.[478]

Since that time, Joe Aillet Stadium has evolved. A luxury skybox was added in 1985, and 7,600 seats were added in 1989 to currently seat 30,918. Artificial turf arrived in 2006. The FieldTurf Mono was replaced in 2008 with the athletic department logo before FieldTurf Revolution was installed in 2015, the current field surface. A twenty-five-by-forty-five-foot videoboard was installed in 2009, referred to as the "Dawgzilla" and "Dooleytron" by Tech fans, in honor of then head coach Derek Dooley. The Davison Athletic Complex, named after the James Davison family, was constructed in the south end zone in 2015. Later improvements have included a new press box, stretching from 10-yard line to 10-yard line, and several renovations within the stadium. The home coaching booths were named after Coach Lewis and his wife, Patsy, in 2017. Historic events have been enjoyed by different generations of Tech fans from the late '60s down to the present in Joe Aillet Stadium.[479] A north end zone project is currently being planned.

Aillet would be remembered after his death for his football knowledge, execution and philosophy. Inside the Charles Wyly Athletic Complex, a piece of his legacy remains on a wall outside the training room: a picture of Aillet beside the Shakespearean quote "To thine own self be true."[480]

When George Doherty became the head coach at Northwestern the year after Joe Aillet died, he took another opportunity to thank his old mentor. Recalling how he worked closely with Aillet, he had called Ruby Aillet as soon as he knew he would get the job because he wanted to tell her before she saw it in the papers. His ability to recruit was developed by observing Aillet: "He gets a lot of the credit for my success, both as a player and as a coach. This individual had more influence on my life than any man I know."[481]

Ruby remained good friends with the Dohertys, presenting him with a silver plaque at George Doherty Night, thrown in his honor on his opening game as head coach of the Demons. "This is one night I wouldn't miss for anything. He is most deserving, and we wish him well."[482]

Further honors and recognitions came frequently as his legacy has been remembered throughout the decades since his death. In 1973, he was inducted into the LSWA Hall of Fame along with Paul "Tank" Younger of Grambling and Bob Pettit of LSU, all unanimously accepted.[483] "It was no accident that major college coaches always looked on Joe and his team with respect," said Jack Fiser, former Louisiana Tech Sports Information director and then head of the *Alumni News* of LSU. "He long insisted on maintaining membership in the NCAA and personally participating in the NCAA's affairs. He was included in its councils and won friends for his institution. Perhaps more importantly, he always subjected his athletic teams to the NCAA's rules even when it pinched."

"We're all so thankful for the nice things said about Joe," Ruby said. "I just wish he were here with us."[484]

The Scholastic Award, previously one of several awards bestowed to players at the Rotary Club Banquet, was renamed the Joe Aillet Scholastic Award in his honor and has over time evolved into the Joe Aillet Endowed Scholarship.[485]

In 1974, Aillet was selected to the Hall of Fame of the National Association of Collegiate Directors of Athletics. In accepting the award, Athletic Director Lambright acknowledged, "Even now Joe Aillet has brought more recognition to Louisiana Tech through his creative and dedicated efforts, and it was a great honor for me to accept the award in his name in Montreal."[486]

Louisiana Tech University honored Joe Aillet in 1983, inducting him in the first class of the Tech Hall of Fame at the second-ranked Lady Techster basketball game against top-ranked USC. Joining him were his former players Garland Gregory and Terry Bradshaw. Other inductees included Jackie Moreland and Maxie Lambright, as well as other Tech legends Atley Donald and Pam Kelly. "I certainly feel that our selection committee had done an excellent job with our first inductees and that each represents the very highest ideals upon which Louisiana Tech University athletics is based," said President Taylor. "Each excelled in his or her field of endeavor and set a high standard for Tech athletics and for this Hall of Fame.[487] These are Tech stars for all seasons, and we want to honor them suitably and permanently."[488]

Ruby, Bobby and Cynthia Aillet showing Joe Aillet's posthumous NACDA award. *From the Louisiana Tech Sports Communication Department.*

Athletic Director Bob Vanatta identified Coach Aillet as "truly a coaching and motivational genius."[489]

Joe Aillet was elected to the National Football Foundation's Hall of Fame in 1989. The most recent toast to his career came from the place it all started. Aillet and Lynch were part of the 2018 class of the Holy Cross Sports Hall of Fame.

While the Quarterback Club existed during Coach Aillet's coaching days and included townspeople of Ruston, the National Association for the Advancement of Grandstand Quarterbacks was formed by former players from the World War II and early '50s years. "You've got to understand that nobody set out to say that we were ever going to meet annually, or that we'd even have a name," said Bobby Aillet. "This is just friends who got together one year—and kept going. Like most things, it just sort of happened." Developed of their own initiative, it started in 1949 when they decided to all make one Tech game each season to meet and reminisce. More and more players were invited, and soon fishing trips, parties, shopping dates, golf and couples-only vacations grew the society into one composed of lifelong friendships. Leo Sanford became the unofficial chair of the association, checking on everybody and keeping them up to date, up to the present. "It's a great group of people to be around," he said.[490]

Bobby would remain involved in football after fully retiring from officiating and his three years as a press box observer. Like his father, he joined a bowl selection committee, this time for the Independence Bowl in Shreveport. At the same time, he was awarded the Contribution to Amateur Football Award as part of the 1990 Independence Bowl ceremonies.[491] In 2005, he was chosen for the Harris Interactive College Football Poll, tasked with ranking NCAA teams and arranging major bowl selections.[492]

Cynthia Aillet's children and grandchildren carried on the Bulldog football and golf coaching tradition. One son, Johnny, got a scholarship to Northwestern State. When he played at the State Fair, some of the Ruston fans cheered for him in remembrance of the time he spent playing football at Ruston High.

As another athlete in the family, Cynthia mostly enjoyed swimming. It is no surprise that she majored in music. Some of her favorite memories of her father involved singing with him. He taught her how to stay composed when singing. One of her highest compliments came when she sang for a group of Tech students while still in high school. The instructor pointed out her composure while singing to the class, telling them how they could learn something from her performance. Whenever her father would play a certain note on the piano, that was her indication that he was about to play one of their songs. She would stand beside him and sing as he played the piano, at home and at social events.

Aillet was the kind of patient family man Cynthia knew she could count on. One time when she was in grade school at A.E. Phillips Lab School, there was something bothering her. Aillet's secretary interrupted a meeting to tell him his daughter needed him. Leaving the men in the room, he brought her into his room so she could tell him what was the matter. She knew that she could have done that more often than she did but did not want to abuse the confidence of her father.[493]

According to a 1969 Tech brochure, Coach Aillet "[b]elongs to that small, elite group which actually gave as much to athletics as he received. Probably he gave more, except that from his own conversation you realize his work

The Aillet family, along with President Taylor and Athletic Director Maxie Lambright, present a portrait of Joe Aillet. *From the Louisiana Tech Sports Communication Department.*

with young men in athletics has brought him a lifetime of happiness through motivated association."[494]

He was also remembered in a *Tech Talk* piece in tribute to him at his passing: "On cold crisp autumn mornings he continues to live as the specter of his remembrance softly calls with the crackle of every leaf on this campus that he loved with every fiber of his soul. And it calls on every Saturday night as his legacy quietly moves through the confines of the stadium that bears his name."[495]

As a child who had traveled from a New York orphan train to a home in Louisiana, Aillet always knew that he was fortunate. Any number of things could have gone wrong. He was thankful for his Youngsville family and chose to embrace his identity even when he found out he was adopted. His grace made him the man who affected so many other lives.

"Cynthia, I'm sorry I don't have more of these grandparents for you," he told her one time when she was visiting those on the Comeaux side. "Dad, that's just not anything you need to worry about," she said. "You're all that I need from your part of the family."

Always a private man, he did not tell anyone, not even his wife, about his adoption until stories started circulating during his illness. Much about his

A late picture of Joe Aillet. *From the Louisiana Tech Sports Communication Department.*

life remains partially known, and it is likely that no one will ever know the entirety of his story on this earth. His earliest memories that he shared with his family, however, shed some light on the infamous train ride. While he was playing in a garden, a sister in her habit came to him. "Come, Joe. It's time to go on your trip. You're going on a train. You might get to find your parents."[496] He remembered later being on a flatboat going over water, which he thought might have been a ferry somewhere in Louisiana. He would go on to become Joseph Rouget Aillet and, under the care of Mrs. Aillet, Father Rouget and the Congregation of Holy Cross, develop into the man he was meant to be.

Coach Aillet's never-give-up attitude was taken up by so many people he influenced. His memory will never die and continues to live on through those who knew him, those who have read of him and the institutions that he clung to.

NOTES

Chapter 1

1. Cynthia Aillet Murry interview, 2019.
2. National Orphan Train Complex, "New York Foundling Hospital," https://orphantraindepot.org/history/the-new-york-foundling-hospital.
3. Andrea Warren, "The Orphan Train," *Washington Post*, last modified 1998, https://www.washingtonpost.com/wp-srv/national/horizon/nov98/orphan.htm.
4. National Orphan Train Complex, New York Foundling Hospital.
5. Alton E. Broussard, "'Baby Train' Festive Occasion in Local History," *Lafayette Daily Advertiser*, Sunday, December 19, 1971, 27; Dianne Creagh, "The Baby Trains: Catholic Foster Care and Western Migration, 1873–1929," *Journal of Social History* 46, no. 1 (2012): 208.
6. Opelousas Orphan Train Museum video, Martha Aubert.
7. Opelousas Orphan Train Museum video, Martha Aubert.
8. Cynthia Aillet Murry interview, 2019.

Chapter 2

9. Cynthia Aillet Murry interview, 2019.
10. *Gold and Blue*, Holy Cross yearbook, 1923.

11. Reverend Jean Proust, Sanctuaire Basile Moreau, "Congregation of Holy Cross," https://www.sanctuairebasilemoreau.org/en/notre-dame-de-sainte-croix-2.
12. Holy Cross High School, Brother Walter Irvin Davenport, CSC, MA, archivist.
13. Reverend Basil Moreau, Circular Letter 36, April 15, 1849.
14. Mike Baiamonte, head football coach of Holy Cross School; Tony Stolz, school historian; Doug Degan, school historian, Holy Cross Sports Hall of Fame.
15. *Gold and Blue*, Holy Cross yearbook, 1923.
16. *The Football History Dude*, "How Football Became Football with Timothy P. Brown," podcast, Sports History Network, sportshistorynetwork.com.
17. Brother Martin, "1922: Quick Fall," Crusader Sports History, https://www.brothermartin.com/blog/wp-content/uploads/SportsHistory/footballhistory/football1922-3.htm.
18. Gordon Rebert, "Jesuits Aerial Attack and Experience Defeats Game Holy Cross Team," *Times-Picayune*, 1922, via http://www.bluejaystigers.com/1920s/1922.htm.

Chapter 3

19. William H. Dunn, CSC, *A Centennial History* (Austin, TX: St. Edward's University Press, 1986), 2–14, https://stedwards.figshare.com/articles/journal_contribution/Saint_Edward_s_University_A_Centennial_History/2004042.
20. *St. Edward's Tower*, St. Edward's College yearbook, 1925, 78.
21. J.W. Halm, "Aillet," *St. Edward's Echo*, vol. 5, no. 3, ed. 1, December 1923, 5, https://texashistory.unt.edu/ark:/67531/metapth891906, University of North Texas Libraries, Portal to Texas History, crediting St. Edward's University.
22. *St. Edward's Echo*, vol. 5, no. 3, ed. 1, "Campus Notes," December 1923, 10, https://texashistory.unt.edu/ark:/67531/metapth891906, University of North Texas Libraries, Portal to Texas History, crediting St. Edward's University.
23. F. James Kinane, "St. Edward's 7—Baylor Cubs 2," *St. Edward's Echo*, vol. 5, no. 1, ed. 1, October 1923, 10, https://texashistory.unt.edu/ark:/67531/metapth891857, University of North Texas Libraries, Portal to Texas History, crediting St. Edward's University.

24. *St. Edward's Echo*, vol. 5, no. 3, ed. 1, "U. of T. Trounced by St. Edward's 35–7," December 1923, 9, https://texashistory.unt.edu/ark:/67531/metapth891906, University of North Texas Libraries, Portal to Texas History, crediting St. Edward's University.

25. *St. Edward's Echo*, vol. 5, no. 3, ed. 1, "What Others Think About Us," December 1923, 9, https://texashistory.unt.edu/ark:/67531/metapth891906, University of North Texas Libraries, Portal to Texas History, crediting St. Edward's University.

26. Stephen V. Rice, "Pinkey Whitney," Society for American Baseball Research, https://sabr.org/bioproj/person/pinkey-whitney/#sdendnote12sym.

27. *St. Edward's Echo*, vol. 6, no. 1, ed. 1, "Athletics," October 1924, 10, https://texashistory.unt.edu/ark:/67531/metapth891778, University of North Texas Libraries, Portal to Texas History, crediting St. Edward's University.

28. Robert Snell, "St. Edward's 28—Louisiana Poly, 12," *St. Edward's Echo*, vol. 6, no. 3, ed. 1, December 1924, 11, https://texashistory.unt.edu/ark:/67531/metapth891787, University of North Texas Libraries, Portal to Texas History, crediting St. Edward's University.

29. *Ruston Daily Leader*, vol. 36, no. 224, "Blue Hogg, Tech Freshman Coach, Holds Unique Record," Thursday, December 14, 1939, 1.

30. Robert Snell, "St. Edward's 35—Tulsa University, 7," *St. Edward's Echo*, vol. 6, no. 3, ed. 1, December 1924, 12, https://texashistory.unt.edu/ark:/67531/metapth891787, University of North Texas Libraries, Portal to Texas History, crediting St. Edward's University.

31. F. James Kinane, "Baylor University 30—St. Edward's 7," *St. Edward's Echo*, vol. 6, no. 3, ed. 1, December 1924, 13, https://texashistory.unt.edu/ark:/67531/metapth891787, University of North Texas Libraries, Portal to Texas History, crediting St. Edward's University.

32. *St. Edward's Echo*, vol. 6, no. 5, ed. 1, "Campus Notes," February 1925, 10, https://texashistory.unt.edu/ark:/67531/metapth891831, University of North Texas Libraries, Portal to Texas History, crediting St. Edward's University; Karen Langley, "ND Nurtures New Orleans Ties," Observer, Thursday, October 17, 2005, https://ndsmcobserver.com/2005/10/nd-nurtures-new-orleans-ties.

33. *St. Edward's Echo*, vol. 6, no. 4, ed. 1, "Joe Aillet," January 1925, 11, https://texashistory.unt.edu/ark:/67531/metapth891859, University of North Texas Libraries, Portal to Texas History, crediting St. Edward's University.

34. *St. Edward's Echo*, vol. 6, no. 4, ed. 1, "Basketball," January 1925, 16, https://texashistory.unt.edu/ark:/67531/metapth891859, University of

North Texas Libraries, Portal to Texas History, crediting St. Edward's University.

35. *St. Edward's Echo*, vol. 6, no. 5, ed. 1, "Saint Edward's 17—San Marcos 31," February 1925, 12, https://texashistory.unt.edu/ark:/67531/metapth891831, University of North Texas Libraries, Portal to Texas History, crediting St. Edward's University.

36. *St. Edward's Echo*, vol. 6, no. 5, ed. 1, "Saint Ed's 24—Simmons, 17" and "St. Ed's 29—Simmons 17," February 1925, 12, https://texashistory.unt.edu/ark:/67531/metapth891831, University of North Texas Libraries, Portal to Texas History, crediting St. Edward's University.

37. *St. Edward's Echo*, vol. 6, no. 6, ed. 1, "St. Edward's vs Stephen F. Austin, and Second Game," March 1925, 11, https://texashistory.unt.edu/ark:/67531/metapth891739, University of North Texas Libraries, Portal to Texas History, crediting St. Edward's University.

38. *St. Edward's Echo*, vol. 7, no. 1, ed. 1, October 1925.

39. Cynthia Aillet Murry interview, 2019.

40. *St. Edward's Echo*, "Varsity Scores Victory Over Tenn. Physicians on Medics' Own Field," 10, in possession of Cynthia Aillet Murry.

41. *St. Edward's Echo*, vol. 7, no. 4, ed. 1, "Joe Aillet," January 1926, 13.

Chapter 4

42. *L'Acadien*, Southwestern Louisiana Institute yearbook, 1927.

43. *The Vermilion*, vol. 23, no. 6, "Bulldogs Defeat Choctaws 20–16," Saturday, December 11, 1926.

44. *The Vermilion*, vol. 23, no. 3, "S.L.I. Stadium Opens Up with Victory," Thursday, October 19, 1926.

45. *L'Acadien*, Southwestern Louisiana Institute yearbook, 1927.

46. 2007 Ragin Cajuns Football Media Guide, "UL Football History: The Story Behind the Nickname," Section 7A, https://static.ragincajuns.com/custompages/mediaguidepdfs/football/2007/section7a.pdf.

47. Louisiana Tech University Student Government Association website, "Legend of the Bulldog."

48. *Ruston Daily Leader*, "Aillet Banquet Set Saturday," Tuesday, June 9, 1970, 5.

49. Cynthia Aillet Murry interview, 2019.

Chapter 5

50. A.L. Williams interview, 2020.

51. *Ruston Daily Leader*, "Aillet Found Fortune While at Haynesville," Friday, June 7, 1970, 7.

52. *Haynesville News*, vol. 7, no. 47, "Many Local Football Fans Attend Game at Winnfield," Thursday, October 6, 1927, 1.

53. *Haynesville News*, vol. 8, no. 44, "New Athletic Field Being Fenced This Week," Thursday, October 11, 1928.

54. *Haynesville News*, vol. 9, no. 43, "Learn More About Football Rules," Thursday, October 3, 1929.

55. *Haynesville News*, vol. 8, no. 36, "Football Season Will Open Here Friday P.M.," Thursday, September 21, 1933, 1.

56. *Haynesville News*, vol. 8, no. 37, "Coach Would Show Plays of Tornado," Thursday, September 28, 1933, 1.

57. *Haynesville News*, vol. 9, no. 39, "Haynesville Schools Open Monday; All Arrangements Made," Thursday, September 5, 1929.

58. *Haynesville News*, vol. 12, no. 29, "Coach Aillet Is Attending School at Texas College," Thursday, July 20, 1932.

59. *Haynesville News*, vol. 13, no. 47, "Tornado, Byrd, Bossier Will Be in Playoff," Thursday, December 7, 1933, 1.

60. *Haynesville News*, "Haynesville Loses State Game at Magnolia," December 8, 1927.

61. *Haynesville News*, vol. 14, no. 46, "Tornado to Play Lafayette Here Thanksgiving Day," Thursday, November 29, 1934, 1.

62. *Haynesville News*, vol. 14, no. 46, "Game Thursday Dedicated to Coach Aillet," Thursday, November 29, 1934, 1.

63. *Haynesville News*, vol. 10, no. 4, "Hotel Manager Compliments Members of the Golden Tornado Team," Thursday, January 2, 1930, 1.

64. *Haynesville News*, vol. 10, no. 5, "Golden Tornado Football Team Honored with Turkey Dinner," Thursday, January 9, 1930, 1.

65. *Haynesville News*, vol. 13, no. 47, "High Tribute Paid Tornado by Hotel Man," Thursday, December 7, 1933, 1.

66. *Haynesville News*, vol. 16, no. 5, "Coach Aillet Is Honored by the Lions Club Wed.," Thursday, January 30, 1936, 1.

67. *Haynesville News*, vol. 16, no. 5, "Aillet Presents Plaques to School," Thursday, January 30, 1936.

68. Hunter Bower, *Haynesville Football: A History of Louisiana's Winningest High School Football Program* (N.p., August 10, 2019), 35.

69. *Ruston Daily Leader*, "Student of Coach Will Match Squad Against Tech Team," Thursday, October 30, 1947, 5.

70. 2011 Haynesville Football Media Guide, http://media.hometeamsonline.com/photos/football/GOLDENTORNADO/2011HAY-CC.pdf.

71. *Tech Talk*, "Hall of Fame Award to Honor Coach Joe Aillet," December 4, 1959, 3.

Chapter 6

72. Cynthia Aillet Murry interview, 2019.

73. *Current Sauce*, vol. 24 no. 3, "Demons and East Texas Lions Clash Today," Saturday, October 31, 1936, 1.

74. *Louisiana Potpourri*, Louisiana Normal 1938 yearbook, 98.

75. *Ruston Daily Leader*, "Joe Aillet—Molder of Teams and Men," Monday, June 28, 1976, 64.

76. *Current Sauce*, vol. 26, no. 9, "Stars of T.C.U. Pass Through," Thursday, January 12, 1939, 5.

77. Cynthia Aillet Murry interview, 2019.

78. *Current Sauce*, vol. 24, no. 15, "Turpin to Go to L.S.U.," Thursday, April 22, 1937, 3.

79. *Current Sauce*, vol. 26, no. 8, "Walter Ledet Honored by Selection on All-S.I.A.A. Eleven," Thursday, December 15, 1938, 5.

80. *Current Sauce*, vol. 27, no. 7 "Business Men to Honor Normal Grid Squad," Thursday, December 14, 1939, 1.

81. *Current Sauce*, vol. 27, no. 1, "Demons Smash Centenary, 15–0," Thursday, September 21, 1939, 1.

82. *Current Sauce*, vol. 27, no. 8, "Dean and Students Are Victims of Holiday Accidents," Thursday, January 11, 1940, 1.

83. *Current Sauce*, vol. 27, no. 5, "Anderson Says," Thursday, November 16, 1939, 1.

Chapter 7

84. Cynthia Aillet Murry interview, 2019.

85. *Current Sauce*, vol. 27, no. 5, "Local Newman Club Installs Chapter at Louisiana Tech Campus," Thursday, November 16, 1939, 1.

86. *Ruston Daily Leader*, vol. 37, no. 209, "Catholic Church Will Be Built," Friday, November 15, 1940, 1.

87. *Tech Talk*, vol. 15, no. 22, "Catholic Church Being Constructed Near Tech Campus," March 14, 1941, 1.

88. *Chronicle of St. Thomas Aquinas Friary*, Archives of the Province of the Sacred Heart, Father Severin Nelles, OFM.

89. *Tech Talk*, vol. 15, no. 25, "Catholic Church to Be Dedicated Friday, May 30," April 11, 1941, 1.

90. *Ruston Daily Leader*, vol. 39, no. 69, "Catholic Ladies Plan Library Opening," Friday, August 28, 1942, 1.

91. *Chronicle of St. Thomas Aquinas Friary*.

92. *Ruston Daily Leader*, vol. 39, no. 257, "WAACs to Observe Memorial Day at Catholic Church," Thursday, May 27, 1943, 1.

93. *Chronicle of St. Thomas Aquinas Friary*.

94. Cynthia Aillet Murry interview, 2019.

95. *Ruston Daily Leader*, vol. 73, "Bishop Opens Piatt Center," Monday, February 5, 1968, 1.

96. Cynthia Aillet Murry interview, 2019.

Chapter 8

97. *Tech Talk*, "Michael Presents 'Souvenir' Ball to '42 Squad," April 24, 1942, 3.

98. *Ruston Daily Leader*, "Heads-Up Play by Bulldogs Is Lauded by Aillet," Thursday, November 1, 1951, 3.

99. *Ruston Daily Leader*, "You Can't Beat Tech's Anderson for Good Playing," Tuesday, September 28, 1954, 3.

100. *Tech Talk*, "Tech Wins All-Sports Trophy for GSC Athletic Supremacy," May 22, 1959, 5.

101. *Ruston Daily Leader*, vol. 37, no. 33, "5 Colleges Plan to Meet at La. Tech Sat.," Tuesday, May 8, 1940, 1.

102. Pat Garrett interview, 2020.

103. *Tech Talk*, "LIC Officials Rap 'Unethical' Moves by League Members," December 13, 1940, 3.

104. *Tech Talk*, "GSC Pro Athletes Will Be Prohibited from Circuit Play," December 10, 1948, 5.

105. *Tech Talk*, vol. 23, no. 29, "Aillet Re-Elected President of GSC by Loop Officials," May 20, 1949, 1.

106. *Ruston Daily Leader*, "Gulf States Conference Will Sponsor Basketball Championship to Name Champs," Wednesday, December 6, 1950, 6.

107. Jim Goodwin, "Bulldog Bites," *Tech Talk*, March 29, 1963, 5.

108. *Ruston Daily Leader*, "Harry Turpin to Be Honorary Referee for GSC Cinderfest," April 28, 1969, 5.

109. *Ruston Daily Leader*, "Honorary Referee," Friday, May 7, 1971, 3.

110. *Tech Talk*, vol. 14, no. 20, "Coach Aillet to Tutor State All-Star Team in Annual Contest," February 23, 1940, 1.

111. *Tech Talk*, vol. 25, no. 1, "Bulldogs Seek Revenge in Opening Grid Game," September 22, 1950, 1.

112. *Tech Talk*, "Press Box Given Superior Rating by Sports Men," April 20, 1951, 5.

113. *Ruston Daily Leader*, "Rally Association to Classify North Louisiana Schools," Friday, December 9, 1949, 1.

114. *Ruston Daily Leader*, "10 High Schools Will Send 41 Golfers Here for Tourney Friday," April 24, 1952, 4.

115. *Ruston Daily Leader*, vol. 70, "Local Institutions Allocated $3,196,044 for Construction," Wednesday, December 22, 1965, 5.

116. *Ruston Daily Leader*, "Tech to Begin Spring Training Here Tuesday," Monday, January 31, 1966, 3.

117. *Tech Talk*, "Tech Grid Mentor Optimistic Over Football Rules Changes," 1940, 3.

118. L.J. Fox, "Diamond Dope," *Ruston Daily Leader*, Tuesday, September 29, 1953, 6.

119. *Ruston Daily Leader*, "45 Report for Spring Grid Work at Tech for Next Four Weeks," Friday, February 6, 1953, 6.

120. Charles W. Tucker Jr., "1960 Rules Changes," *Ruston Daily Leader*, Monday, September 19, 1960, 5.

121. *Ruston Daily Leader*, "Rules Put New Look on Collegiate Football," Wednesday, September 11, 1963.

122. John Ralston, "Bulldog Bites," *Tech Talk*, October 15, 1965, 5.

123. *Ruston Daily Leader*, "Bulldog Football Practice to Commence This Week," Wednesday, February 1, 1965, 3.

124. *Tech Talk*, "Football Scrimmage on Saturday Will Conclude Spring Practice," March 5, 1965, 5.

125. *Ruston Daily Leader*, "Coach Aillet Named to Football Hall of Fame Committee," Wednesday, April 13, 1955, 5.

126. *Ruston Daily Leader*, "Coach Aillet Named to High Position in Midget Football," Friday, July 23, 1955, 8.

127. *Ruston Daily Leader*, "Coach Aillet Gets National Football Group Appointment," Friday, February 17, 1956, 4.

128. *Tech Talk*, "Tech Athletic Director Named to Membership on College Rating Board," September 26, 1958, 7.

129. Program Outline, Ark-La-Tex Sports Award Banquet Athletic Affairs Committee, Shreveport Chamber of Commerce, February 10, 1961.

130. *Tech Talk*, "Coach Aillet Appointed to Coaches' Committee to Pick Award Winner," May 17, 1963, 5.

131. *Tech Talk*, "NAIA Names Stellar Lineman to Hall of Fame," January 11, 1957, 5.

132. *Ruston Daily Leader*, vol. 64, "Joe Aillet Joins NAIA Hall of Fame," Friday, November 27, 1959, 1.

133. Buddy Davis, "Talking Sports," *Ruston Daily Leader*, Wednesday, January 20, 1965, 3; Thomas Aswell, "Aillet Was 'Inspiration' to Athletes," *Shreveport Times*, December 29, 1971, 23.

134. *Tech Talk*, "GSC Commissioner, NCAA Membership Sought for League," April 23, 1965, 5.

135. *Ruston Daily Leader*, "A Day to Be Remembered," Monday, October 14, 1963, 2.

136. *Ruston Daily Leader*, vol. 67, "8,500 See Joe Aillet Ceremonies," Monday, October 14, 1963, 1.

137. Alec Mize interview, 2021.

Chapter 9

138. *Ruston Daily Leader*, vol. 36, no. 219, "Joe Aillet Named Athletic Director," Friday, December 8, 1939, 1.

139. *Tech Talk*, vol. 14, no. 13, "Aillet and Crowley, New Tech Coaches, to Start Work Soon," December 15, 1939, 1; Cynthia Aillet Murry interview, 2019.

140. *Tech Talk*, "Aillet and Crowley, New Tech Coaches."

141. Cynthia Aillet Murry and John Sachs interviews, 2020 and 2021.

142. Cynthia Aillet Murry interview, 2019.

143. *St. Edward's Tower*, St. Edward's College yearbook, 1925; *St. Edward's Echo*, student newspaper, 1924.

144. Cynthia Aillet Murry interview, 2019.

145. John Sachs interview, 2021.

146. Alec Mize interview, 2021.

147. Keith Prince, "Coach Jim Mize: Truth and Honesty Matter the Most," *Monroe News-Star*, Tuesday, July 12, 2005, 3 C.

148. Tom Hinton interview, 2020.

149. Bill Cox interview, 2020.

150. *Tech Talk*, "Coach Aillet Elected by Student Senate," November 7, 1941, 4.

151. John Sachs interview, 2021.

152. Joe Raymond Peace interview, 2020.

153. Billy Jack Talton interview, 2020.

154. Richie Golmon interview, 2020.

155. Jerry Griffin interview, 2020.

156. "He Always Cared," scrapbook in possession of Cynthia Aillet Murry.

157. *Ruston Daily Leader*, vol. 36, no. 221, "Cecil Crowley to Join Tech Staff as Assistant Coach; Aillet to Come Here Dec. 16," Monday, December 11, 1939, 1, Haynesville book.

158. *Ruston Daily Leader*, vol. 67, "Joe Aillet History Is Colorful Story," Friday, October 11, 1963, 1.

159. Leo Sanford interview, 2020.

160. Jimmy Watson, "Continuing a Legacy," *Shreveport Times*, 1, Scrapbook in possession of Cynthia Aillet Murry.

161. Pat Garrett interview, 2020.

162. Billy Jack Talton interview, 2020.

163. Joe Raymond Peace interview, 2020.

164. Jimmy Watson, "Fair Park's Clem Henderson Passes," *Shreveport Times*, March 9, 2015.

165. A.L. Williams interview, 2020.

166. Mickey Slaughter interview, 2020.

167. Wiley Hilburn Jr., "Tech Loses Star to Pro Baseball," *Ruston Daily Leader*, vol. 64, June 4, 1959, 1.

168. J.W. Slack interview, 2020.

169. Flo Miskelly interview, 2020.

170. Bret H. McCormick, "Miskelly's Service Nears End," *Ruston Daily Leader*, Sunday, August 7, 2005, 11A.

171. Prince, "Coach Jim Mize."

172. Alec Mize interview, 2021.

173. E.J. Lewis interview, 2020.

174. Billy Belding interview, 2020.

175. Bil Cox interview, 2020.

176. Holy Cross Hall of Fame, Coach Johnny Lynch.

177. Aillet started officiating high school games in 1953, the same year Lynch became the president and vice-president of the Southeastern Conference Officials as well as the chief referee.

178. *Tech Talk*, "Jolly, Kelly Listed as 1948 Co-Captains of Canine Gridders," January 30, 1948, 3.

179. *Tech Talk*, "Ruston Rotarians Honor Tech Team at Annual Dinner," February 13, 1953, 3.

180. *Tech Talk*, "Grid Squad Elects Rainbolt, Anderson 1955 Co-Captains," December 17, 1954, 4.

181. *Ruston Daily Leader*, vol. 61, "Williams, White, Glover, and Pat Hinton Receive Tech Football Trophies," Thursday, January 17, 1957.

182. L.J. Fox, "Diamond Dope," *Ruston Daily Leader*, Wednesday, January 22, 1958, 4.

183. *Tech Talk*, "Vinyard, Tippit, Lestage Picked as Tri-Captains of 1961 Eleven," February 10, 1961, 6.

184. Cynthia Aillet Murry interview, 2019.

185. A.L. Williams interview, 2020.

186. Aubrey Futrell interview, 2021.

187. Dan Daly, "NFL QBs Knows It's in the Gumbo," *Washington Times*, Thursday, January 29, 2004.

188. *Tech Talk*, "Vinyard, Tippit, Lestage," 6.

189. Alec Mize interview, 2021.

190. *Ruston Daily Leader*, vol. 67, "Tech Players Honored at Banquet," Wednesday, January 22, 1964, 1.

191. *Tech Talk*, "Tech's Championship Footballers Gather Honors at Annual Banquet," February 12, 1965, 5.

192. *Ruston Daily Leader*, vol. 71, "Rotary Club Banquet Honors Tech Athletes," Thursday, January 20, 1966, 1.

193. Prince, "Coach Jim Mize."

194. A transportation route used by the Allied forces to supply Chinese forces against Japan from India.

195. Alec Mize interview, 2021.

196. Bill Cox interview, 2020.

197. *Ruston Daily Leader*, "82 Year Old Mother of Airport Manager Takes First Flight," Monday, June 10, 1946, 1.

198. *Ruston Daily Leader*, "Here and There from the Front Porch of the Airport AD Building," Friday, August 15, 1947, 6.

199. *Ruston Daily Leader*, "Veterans Flock to Airport Under New Training Plan," Tuesday, August 13, 1946, 1.

200. Paul Freeman, "Abandoned and Little-Known Airfields: Northern Louisiana, Ruston Municipal Airport (RSN)," April 15, 2021, http://www.airfields-freeman.com/LA/Airfields_LA_N.htm.

201. *Tech Talk*, vol. 21, no. 17, "Bulldog' Flyers Organize Club; Purchase Plane," November 22, 1946, 1.

202. *Ruston Daily Leader*, "Here and There from the Front Porch," 6.

203. Don Tippit interview, 2020.

204. A.L. Williams interview, 2020.

205. *Ruston Daily Leader*, "LSU's Late Recruiting Criticized by Aillet," Monday, August 28, 1961, 3.

206. Tom Hinton interview, 2020.

207. Paul Hagle, "Bulldog Bites," *Tech Talk*, February 9, 1951, 5.

208. Tom Hinton interview, 2020.

209. Carrell Dowies interview, 2020.

210. *Ruston Daily Leader*, "Coach Aillet Will Have Son of Former Player on '62 Team," July 23, 1962, 6.

211. Nico Van Thyn, "J.W. Slack's Induction into La. Tech Athletic Hall of Fame a Long Time Coming," *Bossier Press-Tribune*, August 28, 2019.

212. Mike Mowad interview, 2020.

213. Joe Comeaux interview, 2020.

214. Leo Sanford interview, 2020.

215. O.K. Davis, "Aillet: More than a Coach," *Ruston Daily Leader*, Wednesday, December 29, 1971, 7.

216. Charlie Bourgeois interview, 2020.

217. Carrell Dowies interview, 2020.

218. Mike Mowad interview, 2020.

219. A.L. Williams interview, 2020.

220. Cynthia Aillet Murry interview, 2019.

221. Dub and Bill Jones interview, 2020.

222. J.W. Slack interview, 2020.

223. *Ruston Daily Leader*, "Joe Aillet—Molder of Teams and Men," 64.

224. Glenn Murphy interview, 2020.

225. Ed Shearer, "Bulldog Bites," *Tech Talk*, October 3, 1958, 6.

226. *Ruston Daily Leader*, "Coach Aillet Describes 1960 Season, 'Unusually Harrowing Experience,'" Wednesday, November 23, 1960, 5.

227. *Ruston Daily Leader*, "Hospitality Shown Tech Commended by Coach Joe," Thursday, November 2, 1961.

228. Billy Jack Talton interview, 2020.

229. Charlie Bourgeois interview, 2020.

230. Don Tippit interview, 2020.

231. Cynthia Aillet Murry interview, 2019.

232. Tom Hinton interview, 2020.

233. A.L. Williams interview, 2020.

234. Billy Jack Talton interview, 2020.

235. Dub and Bill Jones interview, 2020.

236. J.W. Slack interview, 2020.

237. Oland Silk, "Aillet Sparks Memory," *Monroe Star-World*, Thursday, October 15, 1981, 2A.

238. Wallace Martin interview, 2020.

239. A.L. Williams interview, 2020.

240. *Ruston Daily Leader*, vol. 36, no. 262, "Aillet, Crowley Satisfied with Tech Grid Progress," Tuesday, February 6, 1940, 1.

241. William Ekron Bowman, "A Study of the T Formation in Relation to Its Defenses," 1953, via Dissertations, Theses, and Masters Projects, College of William and Mary, Paper 1539624494, https://dx.doi.org/doi:10.21220/s2-3ctq-yh79, 8.

242. Paul Hagle, "Bulldog Bites," *Tech Talk*, February 16, 1951, 5.

243. *Ruston Daily Leader*, "45 Report for Spring Grid Work at Tech for Next Four Weeks," Friday, February 6, 1953, 6.

244. Wiley Hilburn Jr., "Diamond Dope," *Ruston Daily Leader*, Thursday, January 1, 1959.

245. *Tech Talk*, "Tech Installs Pro-Type Offense to Utilize Club's Passing Attack," October 12, 1962, 6.

246. *Ruston Daily Leader*, "Spring Training Starts This Afternoon at Tech," Tuesday, February 5, 1963, 4.

247. *Ruston Daily Leader*, "Sports Chatter," Friday, September 20, 1963, 3.

248. *Ruston Daily Leader*, "Bulldogs Face Upset Possibilities at USL," Wednesday, October 9, 1964, 3.

249. Wallace Martin interview, 2020.

250. Pat Garrett interview, 2020.

251. L.J. Fox, "Diamond Dope," *Ruston Daily Leader*, September 8, 1950, 6.

252. A.L. Williams interview, 2020.

253. *Ruston Daily Leader*, "Football Drills Open Today at Louisiana Tech College," Monday, September 2, 1963, 11.

254. Joel L. Fletcher, "Aillet Retires," *Ruston Daily Leader*, vol. 75, no. 22, Tuesday, June 30, 1970, 1.

255. *Ruston Daily Leader*, "Society," Saturday, August 2, 1941, 3.

256. *Ruston Daily Leader*, "Society," Tuesday, July 28, 1942, 3.

257. *Ruston Daily Leader*, "Tech Coaches Have 17 Former Bulldogs in September Camp," Tuesday, August 16, 1949, 3.

258. *Ruston Daily Leader*, vol. 61, "State Meet for Coaches," Monday, July 29, 1957, 1.

259. *Ruston Daily Leader*, "Prep Clinic Attracts 100 State Mentors," Monday, January 19, 1959, 3.

260. *Ruston Daily Leader*, "Coach Aillet Lecturing at Little Rock," Friday, August 11, 1961.

261. Billy Jack Talton interview, 2020.

262. Louis Bonnette, "Bulldog Bites," *Tech Talk*, February 16, 1962, 5.

263. Glenn Murphy interview, 2020.

264. Alden Reeves interview, 2020.

265. Tommy Linder interview, 2020.

266. Aldon Reeves interview, 2020.

267. Tom Causey interview, 2020.

268. Tom Hinton interview, 2020.

269. Aldon Reeves interview, 2020.

270. Dub and Bill Jones interview, 2020.

271. Billy Belding interview, 2020.

272. Wallace Martin interview, 2020.

273. Dub and Bill Jones interview, 2020.

274. Aubrey Futrell interview, 2021.

275. *Ruston Daily Leader*, vol. 38, no. 127, "Paul Bonin Named Assistant Coach of Tech Freshmen," Tuesday, September 2, 1941, 1.

276. Pete Dosher, "Bulldog Bites," *Tech Talk*, January 14, 1949, 5.

277. Nico Van Thyn, "Once a Knight, Phil and Terry…and 4–16?" Wednesday, June 26, 2013, nvanthyn.blogspot.com.

278. Alec Mize interview, 2021.

279. Cynthia Aillet Murry interview, 2019.

280. Pat Garrett interview, 2020.

281. *Ruston Daily Leader*, vol. 65, "RHS Coach Hoss Garrett Honored with Grid Award," Friday, May 20, 1960, 1.

282. Alec Mize interview, 2020; *Ruston Daily Leader*, vol. 54, "Two New Members Added to Industry Site Purchase Fund," Wednesday, April 6, 1955, 1.

283. Don Tippit interview, 2020.

284. E.J. Lewis interview, 2020.

285. *Ruston Daily Leader*, vol. 37, no. 240, "Dr. Cottingham Will Be Here Tomorrow to Visit Tech Campus and Renew Old Acquaintances," Wednesday, March 5, 1941.

286. *Ruston Daily Leader*, vol. 38, no. 38, "Omega Kappa to Be Installed as Kappa Sigma Chapter Here Today and Tomorrow," Friday, May 16, 1941, 1.

287. Cynthia Aillet Murry interview, 2019.

288. *Tech Talk*, "Coaches and President Ropp Desire to Keep School Spirit High at Tech," January 13, 1950, 4.

289. *Tech Talk*, "President Sees 'Greatest Year' Ahead for Tech," September 28, 1962, 5.

290. *Ruston Daily Leader*, "Tech's Talent Scouts Are Doing Exceptionally Well," Thursday, December 13, 1962, 2.

291. *Tech Talk*, "'Golden Sports Age' Looming at College, Dr. Taylor Declares," January 18, 1963, 3.

292. Kenneth Englade, "Tech Coach Aillet: A David Who Baits Giants Annually," *Ruston Daily Leader*, Thursday, June 30, 1966, 3.

293. Billy Jack Talton interview, 2020.

294. Joe Aillet File, Louisiana Tech Sports Communications Department, Louisiana Tech Sports Information Profile.

295. Louisiana Tech University, "Louisiana Tech to Name Park, Book Atrium for Legendary Leaders," October 7, 2011, latech.edu.

296. Nico Van Thyn, "Once a Knight…The Officials Who Made the Long Run," Wednesday, September 13, 2017, nvanthyn.blogspot.com.

297. Joe Raymond Peace interview.

298. Jerry Griffin interview, 2020.

299. Joe Raymond Peace interview, 2020.

300. Mickey Slaughter interview, 2020.

301. Tom Causey interview, 2020.

302. Billy Jack Talton interview, 2020.

303. Pat Collins interview, 2020.

304. Wallace Martin interview, 2020.

305. Mike Mowad interview, 2020.

306. Kent Heitholt, "Williams Thinking of Players as He Prepares for Last Game," *Shreveport Times*, 5C, scrapbook in possession of Cynthia Aillet Murry.

307. Aubrey Futrell interview, 2021.

308. *Ruston Daily Leader*, "Fans Pay Tribute to Football Star at 'Dub' Jones Dinner Thursday," Friday, August 1, 1952, 3.

309. Dub and Bill Jones interview, 2020.

310. Louisiana Tech University, "ULS President to Serve as Spring Commencement Speaker," April 26, 2018, https://www.latech.edu/2018/04/26/uls-president-to-serve-as-spring-commencement-speaker.

311. *Ruston Daily Leader*, vol. 38, no. 121, "35 Gridders Will Report for Tech Team," Tuesday, August 26, 1941, 1.

312. *Ruston Daily Leader*, vol. 39, no. 11, "Tech Athletes Make Higher Grades than Social Fraternities," Tuesday, June 9, 1942, 1.

313. *Ruston Daily Leader*, vol. 38, no. 171, "Garrett and Aillet Speak to Kiwanians," Thursday, October 23, 1941, 1.

314. *Ruston Daily Leader*, vol. 39, no. 68, "Tech Grid Practice Will Begin Tuesday," Thursday, August 27, 1942, 6.

315. *Ruston Daily Leader*, vol. 39, no. 69, "Fall Football Drills Will Begin Tuesday for Tech Gridmen," Friday, August 28, 1942, 1.

316. Ibid.

317. *Ruston Daily Leader*, vol. 39, no. 78, "Coach Aillet Speaks to Kiwanis," Thursday, September 10, 1942, 3.

318. *Ruston Daily Leader*, vol. 39, no. 118, "Tech Bulldogs Are Primed for S.L.I. Lions Saturday," Friday, November 6, 1942.

319. *Tech Talk*, "Southeastern Lions Face Techmen in Homecoming Tilt," November 6, 1942, 3.

320. Billy Dozier and Buddy Martin, "Bulldog Bites," *Tech Talk*, December 11, 1942, 3.

321. Ibid., December 4, 1942, 3.

322. *Tech Talk*, "Tech Coach Urges State High Schools to Continue Sports," January 15, 1943, 3.

323. *Tech Talk*, vol. 17, no. 17, "Crowley Will Enter Navy on February 11 at Chapel Hill, N.C.," January 29, 1943, 1. Coach Crowley was selected to the V-5 Program as a physical trainer.

324. Cynthia Aillet Murry interview, 2019.

325. *Ruston Daily Leader*, vol. 40, no. 156, "Captain Lockridge Promoted to Major in State Guard Unit," Tuesday, February 29, 1944, 1.

326. *Ruston Daily Leader*, vol. 39, no. 200, "Fifty Men Report for First Meeting of State Home Guard," Tuesday, March 9, 1943, 1.

327. *Ruston Daily Leader*, "Around the Corner," April 10, 1947, 1.

328. *Ruston Daily Leader*, vol. 39, no. 257, "Important Meeting of USO Council to Be Held Tonight at 8," Thursday, May 27, 1943, 1.

329. *Tech Talk*, "Most Tech Athletes of Recent Years Now Wearing Uniforms of USA," August 27, 1943, 3; Cynthia Aillet Murry interview, 2019.

330. *Ruston Daily Leader*, vol. 40, no. 104, "Tech Cancels Plans for Intercollegiate Basketball Team," Wednesday, December 1, 1943, 1.

331. *Ruston Daily Leader*, vol. 41, no. 102, "Tech Football Team 'Shaping Up' Nicely, Says Coach Aillet," Tuesday, August 22, 1944, 1.

332. Wesley Harris, "1944: Navy Saves Small Town College," *Digging the Past*, blog, Friday, December 12, 2014.

333. *Tech Talk*, "13 V-12 Gridders, All Transferred, Will Get Letters," November 24, 1944, 3.

334. *Ruston Daily Leader*, "Tech Grid Captain Names Freida Reed Homecoming Queen," Wednesday, November 7, 6.

335. *Tech Talk*, "Pearce Didier's Heroism in Battle of Belgian Bulge Told by Comrade," September 14, 1945, 3.

336. Billy Jack Talton interview, 2020.

337. Jerry Griffin interview, 2020.

338. Aldon Reeves interview, 2020.

339. Richie Golmon interview, 2020.

340. Wallace Martin interview, 2020.

341. O.K. Davis, "Bradshaw Fires Up Bulldogs," *Ruston Daily Leader*, Tuesday, August 23, 2005, 8.

342. Dub and Bill Jones interview, 2020.

343. *Tech Talk*, "Tech Mascot Killed; Pop to Substitute," October 10, 1941.

344. *Tech Talk*, "Group Appointed by T-Club Head to Buy Bulldog," March 18, 1949, 5.

345. *Tech Talk*, vol. 25, no. 33, "Mascot's Death Reported as Due to Heart Attack," July 13, 1951, 1.

346. *Tech Talk*, "Ten for Tech XI?," February 22, 1952, 2.

347. *Ruston Daily Leader*, vol. 36 no. 249, "Mrs. Joe Aillet Is Severely Injured in Auto Accident," Monday, January 15, 1940, 1; Cynthia Aillet Murry interview, 2019.

348. *Tech Talk*, "Athletic Trainer, Coed Hurt in Auto Wreck," May 17, 1957, 5.

349. *Tech Talk*, "Assistant Coach at Tech, George E. Doherty, Hurt in Crash of Automobiles," December 9, 1960, 5.

350. *Tech Talk*, vol. 15, no. 22, "Dickie Aillet Passes Away in His Sleep," March 14, 1941, 1; Cynthia Aillet Murry interview, 2019.

Chapter 10

351. Pat Garrett interview, 2020.

352. *Ruston Daily Leader*, "Spring Grid Drills End; Tech Coaches 'Pleased,'" Thursday, March 4, 1954, 4.

353. Cynthia Aillet Murry interview, 2019.

354. *Tech Talk*, "11 Tech Gridders Have 2 Bosses: Aillet, Wives," October 3, 1958, 6.

355. Esthman S. Newman, "Prospects for Successful Season for Bulldog Gridders Look Bright but Conference Race to Be Close," *Ruston Daily Leader*, Wednesday, September 9, 1953, 4.

356. Wayne Parker interview, 2020.

357. *Ruston Daily Leader*, "Joe Aillet—Molder of Teams and Men," 64.

358. A.L. Williams interview, 2020.

359. Pat Garrett interview, 2020.

360. Tom Hinton interview, 2020.

361. John Sachs interview, 2021.

362. Billy Jack Talton interview, 2020.

363. Pat Garrett interview, 2020.

364. Billy Jack Talton interview, 2020.

365. Glenn Murphy interview, 2020.

366. *Ruston Daily Leader*, vol. 48, no. 35, "Aillet Tells All," August 22, 1940, 1.

367. *Tech Talk*, vol. 14, no. 24, "Banquet, Game End Spring Work for Grid Players," March 22, 1940, 1.

368. *Ruston Daily Leader*, vol. 37, no. 125, "Lions Hear Blue Note by Aillet," Tuesday, August 27, 1940, 1; *Ruston Daily Leader*, vol. 37, no. 126, "Injuries and Scholastic Troubles Dog Tech Team," Wednesday, August 28, 1940, 1.

369. J.W. Slack interview, 2020.

370. Joe Raymond Peace interview, 2020.

371. O.K. Davis, "George Doherty Had Major Impact on Peace's Career with Bulldogs," *Ruston Daily Leader*, scrapbook in possession of Cynthia Aillet Murry.

372. Billy Jack Talton interview, 2020.

373. A.L. Williams interview, 2020.

374. *Ruston Daily Leader*, "Why Tech's Wall Will Not Crack—Hinton Brothers Are Two Reasons," Friday, October 1, 1954, 5.

375. Tom Hinton interview, 2020.

376. Billy Jack Talton interview, 2020.

377. Dub and Bill Jones interview, 2020.

378. *Ruston Daily Leader*, "Coach Doherty Suffers Attack," Wednesday, July 28, 1965, 5.

379. Dub and Bill Jones interview; *Ruston Daily Leader*, vol. 70, "Coach Aillet Gives Report to Rotarians," Thursday, September 9, 1965, 1.

380. Glenn Murphy interview, 2020.

381. A.L. Williams interview, 2020.

382. Tom Hinton interview, 2020.

383. *Tech Talk*, "Mule Shoe Given Tech by Jonesboro Boosters Brings Luck to Team," October 9, 1953, 5.

384. *Ruston Daily Leader*, "Ladies' Quarterback Club Hears Talk by Coach Aillet," Friday, October 23, 1953, 2.

385. Don Tippit interview, 2020.

386. Carol Dowies interview, 2020.

387. *Ruston Daily Leader*, "Tech Bulldogs Turn Attention Toward Clash with Howard after Saturday Win," Monday, September 17, 1945, 1.

388. Cynthia Aillet Murry interview, 2019.

389. Ibid.

390. Billy Jack Talton interview, 2020.

391. Don Tippit interview, 2020.

392. E.J. Lewis interview, 2020.

393. Alec Mize interview, 2021.

394. *Ruston Daily Leader*, "Dr. Taylor Recalled Year When 'Bear' Paid Tech," Monday, May 24, 1976, 6A.

395. *Ruston Daily Leader*, "'Bear' Paid Tech 25 Grand," Friday, May 7, 1976, 10.

396. *Ruston Daily Leader*, "Joe Aillet—Molder of Teams and Men," 64.

397. *Ruston Daily Leader*, "Joe Aillet History Is Colorful Story," 1.

398. *Ruston Daily Leader*, "Hall of Fame Memories," Wednesday, February 21, 1973, 10.

399. Tom Causey interview, 2020.

400. Ed Shearer, "Bulldog Bites," *Tech Talk*, October 10, 1958, 5.

401. Wallace Martin interview, 2020.

402. Pat Collins interview, 2020.

403. Richie Golmon interview, 2020.

404. "A Moment in Time: Bulldogs Return to Football in 1944," on file, Rick Bryan alumni website.

405. *Tech Talk*, "Tech Ends Season with 7–0 Triumph Over Southwestern," November 24, 1944, 3.

406. *Shreveport Times*, "Two Former Tech-NSU Players Have Total Recall," Friday, October 21, 1977, 4C.

407. Bill McIntyre, "Black Monday: A Bright Beginning for McNew, but Dark for Williams," *Shreveport Times*, scrapbook in possession of Cynthia Aillet Murry.

408. *Shreveport Times*, "Two Former Tech-NSU Players" 4C.

409. McIntyre, "Black Monday."

410. *Tech Talk*, "D'Artois Lauds Tech Behavior at State Fair," November 6, 1964, 4.

411. *Tech Talk*, vol. 40, no. 8, "Fant Commends Student Conduct at State Fair," November 12, 1965, 1.

412. Pete Dosher, "Bulldog Bites," *Tech Talk*, December 3, 1948, 7.

413. Glenn Lewis, "Bulldog Bites," *Tech Talk*, December 4, 1964, 5.

414. *Tech Talk*, "Garland Gregory to Join Physical Education Staff at Tech This December," May 13, 1966, 3.

415. Cynthia Aillet Murry interview, 2019.

416. *Ruston Daily Leader*, vol. 39, no. 71, "45 Candidates Report for Football Practice," Wednesday, September 2, 1942, 1.

417. Glenn Murphy interview, 2020.

418. A.L. Williams interview, 2020.

419. Bobby Henderson, "Bulldog Bites," *Tech Talk*, December 8, 1950, 4.

Chapter 11

420. Cynthia Aillet Murry interview, 2019.

421. *Ruston Daily Leader*, "Women Golfers of Northeast Louisiana Form Association," Wednesday, August 15, 1951, 4.

422. *Tech Talk*, "Bulldog Bites," May 2, 1958, 5.

423. *Tech Talk*, "Roy Nash Loses Bid to Repeat as State Amateur Golf Champ," May 1, 1959, 5.

424. *Tech Talk*, "Tech's Roy Pace Best Amateur in Orleans Open," March 8, 1963, 5.

425. *Tech Talk*, "4 Golf Lettermen Return; To Face Tough Loop Foes," February 22, 1963, 5.

426. *Tech Talk*, "Lyn Fuller Returns as Only Letterman on Tech Golf Squad," March 20, 1964, 5.

427. Esthman S. Newman, "Bulldog Bites," *Tech Talk*, May 23, 1941, 3.

428. Nico Van Thyn, "Once a Knight, 'Smooth Man' Remembered (from June 1973)," Tuesday, May 20, 2014, nvanthyn.blogspot.com.

429. Roy Pace interview, 2021.

Chapter 12

430. *Ruston Daily Leader*, vol. 72, "Joe Aillet Steps Down as Bulldog Mentor," Friday, March 31, 1967, 1.

431. Bill McIntyre, "Hello, Who?," *Shreveport Times*, Friday, March 31, 1967, 1C.

432. *Ruston Daily Leader*, vol. 72, "Professors Commends Joe Aillet," Thursday, April 4, 1967, 1.

433. Bill McIntyre, "Joe Aillet Resigns as La. Tech Football Coach After 26 Seasons; Stays on as Athletic Director," *Shreveport Times*, Friday, March 31, 1967, 1C.

434. Wiley Hilburn Jr., "From the Sidelines," *Ruston Daily Leader*, Tuesday, August 30, 1960, 4.

435. Wiley Hilburn, "Back to Aillet: Best La. Tech Schedule Ever," *Shreveport Times*, Monday, August 9, 2010, 6A.

436. *Tech Talk*, "Maxie Lambright to Arrive Here for Duty May 15," May 5, 1967, 5.

437. Nico Van Thyn, "Once a Knight, Lambright, Part III: Letting the Coaches Coach," Sunday, December 18, 2016, nvanthyn.blogspot.com.

438. *Ruston Daily Leader*, "Aillet on Gridiron Committee," June 21, 1968, 5.

439. *Ruston Daily Leader*, "Tech Joins in 100th Anniversary Observance," September 11, 1969, 5.

440. *Ruston Daily Leader*, "Robertson Pleases Aillet," Thursday, February 23, 1967, 3.

441. *Ruston Daily Leader*, "Klosterman: Bradshaw's the Best," Tuesday, January 13, 1970, 4.

442. Bud Montet, "More than a Coach," *Baton Rouge Morning Advocate*, Wednesday, December 29, 1971, 3C.

443. Cynthia Aillet Murry interview, 2019.

444. O.K. Davis, "Extension Request Sent to Dr. Taylor March 2," *Ruston Daily Leader*, Monday, March 23, 1970, 5.

445. O.K. Davis, "Tech Athletic Head to Retire," *Ruston Daily Leader*, vol. 74, no. 207, Friday, March 20, 1970.

446. *Ruston Daily Leader*, "Aillet Feats to Be Recalled," Monday, June 1, 1970, 7.

447. O.K. Davis, "An Era Ends Saturday," *Ruston Daily Leader*, Thursday, June 11, 1970, 8.

448. *Ruston Daily Leader*, "Aillet Banquet Set Saturday," Tuesday, June 9, 1970, 5.

449. Ibid.

450. O.K. Davis, "From the Press Box," *Ruston Daily Leader*, Monday, June 29, 1970, 6.

451. *Ruston Daily Leader*, "Aillet Banquet Set Saturday," 5.

452. Davis, "Era Ends Saturday," 8.

453. *Ruston Daily Leader*, vol. 75, no. 11, "Joe Aillet Honored at Banquet Saturday," Monday, June 15, 1970, 1.

454. Ibid.

455. J.W. Slack interview, 2020.

456. *Tech Talk*, "Tech Stadium," October 15, 1965, 5.

457. *Ruston Daily Leader*, "75 Years for Tech Athletic Program," Wednesday, February 10, 1971, 10C.

458. *Ruston Daily Leader*, "Tech Paces Grid Club," Monday, September 28, 1970, 6.

459. *Ruston Daily Leader*, "Aillet Cited," Wednesday, October 13, 1971, 3.

460. *Ruston Daily Leader*, vol. 75, no. 62, "Coach Aillet Has Surgery," Wednesday, August 26, 1970, 1.

461. *Ruston Daily Leader*, "Joe Aillet Recovering," Wednesday, March 17, 1971, 7.

462. Davis, "Era Ends Saturday," 8.

463. Cynthia Aillet Murry interview, 2019.

464. *Tech Talk*, "Phillips Drives Athletic Bus 15,000 Miles without Accident," March 7, 1941, 3.

465. *Tech Talk*, "Negro College Helps Bulldogs' Football Travel," December 18, 1942, 3.

466. *Tech Talk*, "Two Negro Elevens to Battle at Tech on Saturday Night," December 6, 1946, 5; NCAA Division II-III Football Records, Special Regular- and Postseason Games, http://fs.ncaa.org/Docs/stats/football_records/D2/2010/SpecialGames.pdf.

467. Richie Golmon interview, 2020; Pat Garrett, *Harps Upon the Willows* (San Antonio, TX: Burke Publishing Company, 1995), 125–27.

468. Bill McIntyre, "In the Harbor," *Shreveport Times*, December 29, 1971.

469. Bill McIntyre, "The 'Coach' Has Retired," *Shreveport Times*, December 29, 1971, 23.

470. O.K. Davis, "Coach Aillet," *Ruston Daily Leader*, vol. 77, no. 202, Wednesday, December 29, 1971, 3.

471. Rick Bryan, "Joe Aillet: Remembering a Legend," on file, from older, now obsolete Tech alumni website.

472. Davis, "Aillet: More than a Coach," 7.

473. Aswell, "Aillet Was 'Inspiration' to Athletes," 23.

474. Ibid.

475. O.K. Davis, "Rotarians Hear Eulogy," *Ruston Daily Leader*, scrapbook in possession of Cynthia Aillet Murry.

476. Alec Mize interview, 2021.

477. *Tech Talk*, vol. 46, no. 11, "Athletic Stadium and Fieldhouse to Be Named for Late Coach Aillet," Thursday, January 6, 1972, 1.

478. O.K. Davis, "Tech Facilities Named for Aillet," *Ruston Daily Leader*, scrapbook in possession of Cynthia Aillet Murry.

479. LA Tech Sports, "Joe Aillet Stadium," https://latechsports.com/facilities/joe-aillet-stadium/4; LA Tech Sports, "Home Coaches Booth to Be Named in Honor of E.J. and Patsy Lewis," May 17, 2017, https://latechsports.com/news/2017/5/11/Home_Coaches_Booth_to_be_named_in_Honor_of_E_J_and_Patsy_Lewis.

480. Scott Beder, "Not the Usual Coach," *Monroe News-Star*, Sunday, August 14, 2005, 3C.

481. "Shoe's on Other Foot for NSU Coach," scrapbook in possession of Cynthia Aillet Murry.

482. *Ruston Daily Leader*, "'Doherty Night' Set Saturday," Wednesday, September 13, 1972, 7.

483. McNeese State University Sports Information Office, Louis Bonnette, July 17, 1972.

484. *Ruston Daily Leader*, "Aillet, Younger, Pettit: Hall Inductees," Tuesday, February 20, 1973, 6.

485. *Ruston Daily Leader*, "Duron, McNeely: Top Bulldogs," Friday, February 1, 1974, 6; LA Tech Alumni, "LA Tech Athletic Club, Joe Aillet Endowed Scholarship," https://www.latechalumni.org/s/810/rd/athletics-interior.aspx?sid=810&gid=1&pgid=1992.

486. *Ruston Daily Leader*, "Joe Aillet Chosen for Hall of Fame," Friday, July 12, 1974, 4.

487. Louisiana Tech Sports Information, "Tech Hall of Fame Induction, January 3, 1984," December 28, 1983.

488. Louisiana Tech Sports Information, "Seven Set for Louisiana Tech Hall of Fame," November 11, 1983.

489. Jim McClain, "Tech Lauds 7 Charter Members," *Shreveport Times*, Wednesday, January 4, 1984, 4C.

490. Teddy Allen, "A War-Born 'Association' Is Still in the Ol' Ballgame," *Monroe News-Star*, Sunday, July 1, 2012, scrapbook in possession of Cynthia Aillet Murry.

491. *Shreveport Times*, "Aillet Picked for Award," scrapbook in possession of Cynthia Aillet Murry.

492. Davis, "Bradshaw Fires Up Bulldogs," 8.

493. Cynthia Aillet Murry interview, 2019.

494. Aswell, "Aillet Was 'Inspiration' to Athletes," 23.

495. Chip Rogers, "Montage," *Tech Talk*, scrapbook in possession of Cynthia Aillet Murry.

496. Cynthia Aillet Murry interview, 2019.

ABOUT THE AUTHOR

Christopher Alan Kennedy is a student in the Master of Library and Information Science program at LSU. He earned a BA in history, minoring in English, at Louisiana Tech University (2018) and a Master of Arts in teaching from LA Tech (2020). He enjoys his current employment as administrative coordinator at the Louisiana State Archives and gaining further experience volunteering at other archives and museums.

Courtesy Daniel Lewis, multimedia specialist of the Louisiana State Archives.

Visit us at
www.historypress.com